BARACK
an american story
OBAMA

By Bob Carlton & Ariele Gentiles

 ZONDERVAN®

ZONDERVAN.com/
AUTHORTRACKER
follow your favorite authors

 youth
specialties

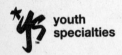

youth specialties

Barack Obama: An American Story
Copyright 2008 by Bob Carlton and Ariele Gentiles

Youth Specialties resources, 300 S. Pierce St., El Cajon, CA 92020 are published by Zondervan, 5300 Patterson Ave. SE, Grand Rapids, MI 49530.

ISBN 978-0-310-67003-2

Web site addresses listed in this book were current at the time of publication. Please contact Youth Specialties via e-mail (YS@YouthSpecialties.com) to report URLs that are no longer operational and replacement URLs if available.

Cover and interior design by Mark Novelli, IMAGO MEDIA

Printed in the United States of America

08 09 10 11 12 13 14 • 20 19 18 17 16 15 14 13 12 11 10 9 8 7 6 5 4 3 2 1

contents ★ ★ ★ ★ ★ ★ ★ ★ ★ ★ ★ ★ ★ ★

INTRODUCTION:
THE FIERCE URGENCY OF NOW

We are now faced with the fact,
my friends, that tomorrow is today.
We are confronted with the fierce
urgency of now.

—MARTIN LUTHER KING JR.

America appeared to be coming apart at the seams. Thousands of miles away, an unpopular war was raging with no end in sight. Economic challenges at home made it difficult for families to make ends meet. The nation's trust in institutions like the church and government had taken a huge hit. Politicians faced a country that appeared on the verge of a second Civil War. Young people were rising up in unprecedented numbers as part of a cultural and political rebellion that took its name from the radical idea of love.

A man climbed some steps to a podium to proclaim an unpopular truth. His skin color subjected him to different treatment in a land founded on freedom and equality. His faith drove him to speak out, no matter the cost:

We are now faced with the fact, my friends, that tomorrow is today. We are confronted with the fierce urgency of now. In this unfolding conundrum of life and history, there is such a thing as being too late. Procrastination is still the thief of time. Life often leaves us standing bare, naked, and dejected with a lost opportunity. The tide in the affairs of men does not remain at flood—it ebbs. We may cry out desperately for time to pause in her passage, but time is adamant to every plea and rushes on. Over the bleached bones and jumbled residues of numerous civilizations are written the pathetic words, "Too late." There is an invisible book of life that faithfully records our vigilance or our neglect.

That man was Dr. Martin Luther King Jr., speaking from the pulpit at the historic Riverside Church in New York City. The year was 1967. The war was the conflict in Vietnam.

America was in the middle of a revolution in civil rights, one that would eventually circle the globe. President Lyndon B. Johnson, responding to the moral leadership of Dr. King and others, had worked to overcome southern resistance (including many religious leaders) and convinced Congress to pass the Civil Rights Act of 1964, outlawing most forms of racial segregation. In 1965 Johnson worked with senators and civil rights leaders to achieve passage of the Voting Rights Act, which outlawed discrimination in voting and allowed millions of southern Blacks to vote for the first time. That same year, after the murder of a prominent civil rights worker, President Johnson went on television to announce the arrest of four Ku Klux Klansmen implicated in her death. He denounced the Klan as a "hooded society of bigots," urging the nation to "return to a decent society before it's too late." Johnson drew on the core themes of Christian redemption to push for civil rights, ultimately mobilizing support from churches North and South. In 1967, Johnson appointed civil rights attorney Thurgood Marshall to the Supreme Court, making Marshall the first African American to serve on the Court.

Five thousand miles away from the White House, a six-year-old boy was living with his mother in Honolulu, Hawaii. He'd been born on this island of mystery and beauty, the child of a white woman from Kansas and a black sheepherder from Kenya. His father had left him and his mother when the boy was two years old, and mother and son had subsisted on the charity of family and friends, as well as assistance from the U.S. government. In 1967, the young mother had recently returned to school for the first time since her divorce. During the next year, the mother would remarry and give birth to another child, and the family of three would move to a country halfway around the world.

No life story is universal, but the journey of this young boy born in the 49th state resonates with the life experience of millions of other young women and men. A boy who works to find his place in a family where he is visibly different from his mother, father, and siblings. A young person living in a distant land, discovering new friends, a new language, and heartbreaking lessons about his identity. A fatherless son struggling to gain a sense of identity and an understanding of how vital parenting is to the families and communities we live in. A young black man struggling for acceptance at institutions of privilege, where he finds himself growing so angry and disillusioned at the world around him that he turns to alcohol and drugs. A searching adult who turns to Jesus for deeper meaning, finding an example that leads him to dedicate his life to feeding the hungry and healing the sick, always prioritizing those his Savior called "the least of these" over the powerful.

Barack Obama has traveled that journey from Hawaii to the cusp of the highest political office in the United States of America. Obama's story is filled with historic "firsts"—from the schools he attended, to the jobs he has taken, to the legislation he has championed. His story is also one of reconciliation: As a son growing up without a father, as an African American in a country that still struggles with racism, as an elected official who struggles to work beyond the stifling boundaries of partisan politics. For this man who loves building bridges and playing basketball, there is no greater calling than that of serving the common good, working to change hearts and change structures.

Forty years after Martin Luther King climbed those steps at the Riverside Church, Barack Obama found himself

★ ★

> I think people are more excited about the potential for more transparency in government. Whether or not that happens remains to be seen.
>
> —LINNI KRAL,
> 19-YEAR-OLD COLLEGE STUDENT

challenged by the fierce urgency of now. After a career in public service, Obama faced a country mired in a war in Iraq, facing mounting economic woes, and experiencing what many saw as a void in leadership. He found himself haunted by King's warning that we dare not wait until it is too late, procrastinating and hoping others might answer the call. If he were to pursue the Democratic nomination for president, Obama knew he was certain to face complaints about his age, his race, his experience, and even his church. But he could not turn away from the fierce urgency of now that pounded in his soul.

On February 10, 2007, a cheering crowd of thousands braved frigid temperatures to gather outside the Old State Capitol in Springfield, Illinois. Built in 1837, this capitol building is where Abraham Lincoln once declared, "A house divided against itself cannot stand." After climbing the steps of this great building that gave America Abraham Lincoln, Barack Obama looked out at the crowd who'd come to hear him announce his long-shot bid for the presidency and spoke these words:

I am not running for this office to fulfill any long-held plans or because I believe it is somehow owed to me. I never expected to be here, and I always knew the journey would be improbable. I've never been on one that wasn't.

I am running because of what Dr. King called "the fierce urgency of now." I am running because I do believe there's such a thing as being too late. And that hour is almost here.

The path Obama has followed in journeying from that announcement in Springfield through his accepting the Democratic nomination for president has been quite unlike that of any previous presidential candidate. Americans are used to voting for presidential candidates with backgrounds as lawyers, military officers, businessmen, career politicians, and even farmers. This is the first time we've been asked to vote for someone who identifies himself primarily as a community organizer. Of course, Barack Obama also has experience as a lawyer, a law professor, and a senator, but throughout the campaign he has frequently referred to the years he spent as a community organizer in Chicago as "the best education I ever had."

No campaign in recent history has relied more on the importance of grassroots organizing. If he's elected president, Obama believes he will have to find a balance between working inside the Beltway and encouraging Americans to organize and mobilize. He has built his campaign on the belief that his ability to reform health care, tackle global warming, and restore job security and decent wages will depend, in large measure, on whether he can use his bully pulpit to mobilize public opinion and encourage Americans to battle powerful corporate interests and members of Congress who resist change. This grassroots campaign has redefined what online politics means, changing the landscape of how individuals can connect, contribute, and work to funnel their energy into a campaign.

Obama's journey to the Democratic nomination has also included an unprecedented level of involvement among young people. "Conventional wisdom has a name for candidates who rely on the youth vote: loser," said George Mason University professor Michael McDonald, an expert on voter turnout, in a recent article in *Time* magazine. "Clearly, this was different." Obama's campaign has ignored this conventional wisdom, turning out voters 25 years of age and younger in record numbers. *The Washington Post* reported in Spring 2008 that:

> While overall Democratic turnout jumped 90% [from 2004], the number of young Democrats participating soared 135%...According to surveys of voters entering the caucuses, young voters preferred Obama over the next-closest competitor by more than 4 to 1.

> Young people are ready to have their voices heard by their candidate. And we would like to think that Barack Obama is our candidate.
>
> —LAURA FRANKEL, 20-YEAR-OLD COLLEGE STUDENT

Political scientist Peter Dreier has observed, "The youngest generation of American voters has chosen a candidate." Dreier notes that Obama's victory in becoming the Democratic nominee "may well be the first in which the youth vote played a decisive role." In a recent post on the online site Huffington Post, Dreier described some of the details of these efforts.

The Obama campaign has put together a sophisticated effort to target young voters on and off college campuses, including hiring student government leaders, activists from recent campus protest movements, and political neophytes. During the summer of 2008, the campaign recruited thousands of college students for a six-week crash course in politics and community organizing in key swing states. Many of them have stayed on with the campaign. Indeed, for many college students and post-college twenty-somethings, the Obama crusade has reached a drop-out-of-school or quit-my-job level of excitement.

An example of the powerful joining of youth and grassroots organizing is 20-year-old Tobin Van Ostern, who finished his sophomore year at George Washington University in the spring of 2008. This fall, Van Ostern is working in the Barack Obama campaign as a full-time organizer. Van Ostern started Students for Obama on his campus last year as a Facebook group. This online organizing tool has spread to chapters on 800 campuses. "There's a young-voter revolution underfoot," Alexandra Acker, executive director of Young Democrats of America, told *The Nation* magazine. Young Democrats of America is one of the many partisan and nonpartisan groups working to expand political involvement among the under-thirty population.

Perhaps most importantly, Obama's story is one that is profoundly rooted in his faith in Jesus Christ. As one supporter has noted, Barack Obama's narrative is one of reconciliation and hope. In his book, *The Audacity of Hope*, Obama writes about what happened to him after he submitted himself to God's will and dedicated himself to discovering God's truth. Obama describes this discernment as an "ongoing process for all of us in making sure that we are living out our faith every day." Obama has consistently pointed to his faith as the primary motivator for his career of working for the common good. In a July 2008 interview with *Newsweek* magazine, Obama spoke to this directly:

I am a big believer in not just words, but deeds and works. I don't believe that the kingdom of God is achievable on Earth without God's intervention, and without God's return through Jesus Christ, but I do believe in improvement.

With his strong rooting in the African-American church, Obama has been able to express his beliefs in a community drenched in religion. Throughout its story in America, the African-American church has found God together as a people, a faith perspective that follows God in the community. This faith tradition has called followers of Jesus to foster a profound sense of community, rather than the individualism and materialism that sometimes marks much of the contemporary church culture.

When asked about Barack Obama's faith, the man identified by many as President Bush's Pastor, Rev. Kirbyjon Caldwell, said this:

> While the differences between President Bush and Senator Obama are very, very clear, allow me to share with you what their commonalities are. One, they have deep, resolute loyalty to their country, to their families, and to their God. They are both Christians. They both love their wives intensely. They're both very good dads. They are also strong believers

in rebuilding the family and rebuilding the infra-structure of our communities...Now, obviously, they have two entirely different approaches as to how to achieve that common good.

Obama was asked by the online site BeliefNet if he had any particular routines or rituals before he takes to a podium for a political speech. His answer pointed to the centrality of faith in his own life:

> The prayer that I tell myself is a fairly simple one: I ask in the name of Jesus Christ that my sins are forgiven, that my family is protected and that I am an instrument of God's will. I'm constantly trying to align myself to what I think he calls on me to do. And sometimes you hear it strongly and sometimes that voice is more muted.

Steeped in a personal history perhaps unique to politics, but by no means uncommon in the eclectic communities stretched across this nation, Barack Obama's life is driven by a strong faith and the same "fierce urgency of now" that Martin Luther King Jr. spoke of four decades earlier. Today, he stands on the cusp of becoming the first African-American president of the United States, eager to lead the country toward a better tomorrow. Guided by a belief that change must start with ordinary citizens and not rich, removed politicians, he is urging all generations to hope—courageously.

HUMBLE BEGINNINGS

**In no other country on earth
is my story even possible.**

—BARACK OBAMA

In the early 1960s, Hawaii was a center of great change. People all over the world came to the state, attracted by the mystery and beauty of this volcanic island chain. Hawaii is made up of hundreds of islands spread over 1,500 miles. It became our 49th state in 1959, one of only four current states that were independent prior to becoming part of the United States. As the new decade dawned, a modern state was emerging with a construction boom and rapidly growing economy.

Barack Obama was born on August 4, 1961, in the state capital of Honolulu, the only son of his parents' short union. His parents met and fell in love at college, as many people do. His father, Barack Obama Sr., was born in 1936 on the shores of Lake Victoria in Nyang'oma Kogelo, Alego, Siaya District, Kenya. The elder Obama grew up herding goats in his native country, but longed for a different life. He won a scholarship from a program offering Western educational opportunities to outstanding Kenyan students. Obama Sr. traveled thousands of miles to Hawaii, where he would study economics at the East-West Center of the University of Hawaii at Manoa. Obama was one of the school's first African students. "He had this very magnetic personality," college friend and Hawaiian congressman Neil Abercrombie recalled in an interview with the *Washington Post*.

The magnetic Obama Sr. attracted the attentions of a young Kansas girl, Ann Dunham, whose family had recently moved to Hawaii. Dunham has been described as a quiet young woman, intelligent and independent, prone to the role of observer. One high school friend commented to the *LA Times*: "If you were concerned about something going wrong in the world, Ann would know about it first...We were liberals before we knew what liberals were." In the same article, another friend called Ann "the original feminist."

Ann Dunham enrolled at the University of Hawaii at Manoa, where she studied anthropology. She and Obama met one another in a Russian language class. They began dating, ignoring the social perceptions of that time regarding interracial relationships. A 1958 Gallup poll showed that 96 percent of white Americans disapproved of interracial marriage, and laws prohibiting interracial relationships were still on the books in 16 states, mostly in the South and the Midwest. By the 1960s civil rights organizations were helping interracial couples that were being penalized for their relationships take their cases to the Supreme Court.

Although Hawaii did not outlaw interracial relationships, they were extremely rare. When Obama and Dunham became engaged, both sets of parents opposed the marriage. Obama Sr.'s father was particularly upset, writing that he "didn't want the Obama blood sullied by a white woman." After discovering Dunham was pregnant, the couple married on February 2, 1961, in a civil ceremony at the courthouse in Maui, Hawaii. Dunham was still just a teenager, only 18 at the time. Barack Obama Jr. was born several months later.

With a young child at home, Dunham made the difficult decision not to return to school. Just a year later, Obama Sr. was offered a scholarship to study toward a doctorate at Harvard University. He left his family in Hawaii with a plan of studying at Harvard and then returning to his Kenyan home to use his education to reinvent the country. Dunham chose not to follow, and when baby Obama was only two years old, his parents signed the divorce papers.

Obama's mother returned to school shortly after her divorce. Balancing college and caring for a young child, Dunham subsisted primarily on food stamps and the loyal aid of friends and family while she completed her degree. During this time, she fell in love again, this time with a young student from Indonesia, Lolo Soetoro. They were married in 1967. The same year, Dunham (now Ann Soetoro) and her son made the move of more than 6,000 miles to her new husband's homeland.

Indonesia was a very different world from Honolulu. Many years later, Barack Obama would recall in his memoir his arrival to the new land with his mother, "Walking off the plane, the tarmac rippling with heat, the sun bright as a furnace. I clutched her hand, determined to protect her." He was just six years old.

The multiethnic family expanded when Barack's half-sister Maya was born. Lolo Soetoro worked for the Indonesian army as a geologist for some time, and then took a job as a government relations consultant with Mobil Oil. Little "Barry," as Barack was known then, adjusted to his new home and quickly made friends with other children, though he and his mother were the first foreigners in their community. Barack began attending classes at a Catholic primary school then transferred to a closer public school. His classes were all in Indonesian, which made it very hard on Obama. Concerned about his education, Obama's mother woke him up before dawn every morning to teach him English because the family couldn't afford the private international school.

Obama's mother also worked hard to help him learn about the U.S. civil rights movement, Martin Luther King Jr., and other African-American figures and activists.

When Obama was 10, his mother sent him back to Hawaii to live with his maternal grandparents, Stanley and Madelyn Dunham. In his book *Dreams from My Father*, Obama described his grandmother as "quiet, yet firm"—in contrast to his "boisterous" grandfather. Obama considered his grandmother "a trailblazer of sorts, the first woman vice president of a local bank in Hawaii." Stanley Dunham had been working in Kansas when Pearl Harbor was bombed in 1941. He immediately enlisted in the army, where he served on the European front in World War II under the leadership of the esteemed General George S. Patton. Obama's grandmother, Madelyn, also did what she could to support the war effort, going to work on a bomber assembly line.

After the war ended Madelyn and Stanley both worked full-time. They struggled to make ends meet, living for a time in California, Kansas, Texas, and Seattle. In 1960 the family moved to Hawaii, where Stanley found a good job working in a furniture store. Madelyn began working at the Bank of Hawaii, and would eventually become one of its vice presidents. Obama has said his grandparents had a profound influence upon his character, teaching him the Midwest virtues of hard work and service to one's country.

Moving back to Hawaii at age 10 was difficult for Obama, but he had the chance to attend the renowned Punahou School on scholarship. Founded in 1841, Punahou School was designed originally to provide a quality education to the children of Congregational missionaries, allowing these young people to stay in Hawaii with their families rather than being sent away to school. The school's first class had only 15 students. The prestigious school draws its name from a local legend: An aged Hawaiian couple lived in Manoa and had to travel far for water. They prayed for a spring. In a dream, they were told to uproot the stump of an old hala tree. When they removed the tree stump, they uncovered a spring of clear, sweet water, which they named Ka Punahou—the New Spring.

It was in his years at this elite private school that Obama first developed an intense appreciation of his multiethnic background (a Kenyan father, a white mother, an Indonesian half-sister) and an acute awareness of racism. Following a pattern that was to mark his life, Obama was one of only three African-American students at Punahou. The racial dynamics of Obama's own experience in Hawaii were quite complicated. Due to his skin color, Obama was perceived as African American by nearly everybody he met. But in living with his grandparents, his own home was a white household. It was at this point in his life that Obama first became conscious of racism and what it means to be an African American. He was also much less affluent than the other students at Punahou School.

★ ★ ★ ★ ★

In 1971, Obama and his father would meet for the first time since his parents' divorce—and it would turn out to be the last time Barack would ever see his father. "He and my mother divorced when I was only two years old, and for most of my life I knew him only through the letters he sent and the stories my mother and grandparents told," Obama said in a speech just before Father's Day in 2008. His father's life in Kenya had taken a tailspin into drinking and poverty, from which he never fully recovered. The elder Obama lost both legs in an automobile accident, and subsequently lost his job. He died not long afterward at the age of 46 in a car crash in Nairobi. Barack Obama Sr. is the main subject of his son's memoir, *Dreams from My Father.*

Any child is greatly affected by the absence of a parent, and Obama was no exception. The experience of being raised in a home without his father had a profound effect on him that would lead him to take his own role as a dad very seriously. These years in Hawaii were especially difficult for him because his mother, too, was not always there. For much of the time, he actually lived with his grandparents, beginning when he first left Indonesia to attend Punahou. After separating from her second husband, Obama's mother rejoined him in Hawaii to study at graduate school. During the years that he lived with his mother, the family slept in a tiny apartment, and their primary source of income was Dunham's student grants. Just a few years later, when Obama was 14, Obama's mother and Maya went back to Indonesia, while Obama decided to remain with his grandparents. Obama has said of this period, "I didn't feel [her absence] as a deprivation, but when I think about the fact that I was separated from her, I suspect it had more of an impact than I know."

Obama has said that this deeply felt conflict during his early teen years led him to act out and rebel. Obama spent a great deal of time in high school on the basketball court—releasing tension, perfecting his game—but gave limited attention to his studies. Though he's not remembered as a great orator or debater by his peers, he did begin developing his writing voice; he even wrote poetry for his school's literary magazine.

Obama has also been quite candid about his engagement in some self-destructive behavior during these years, including his experimenting with alcohol, marijuana, and cocaine during this time of social confusion. He has been very honest about this time in his life, regarding his involvement with those substances as very poor decisions. Many young people today are appreciative of Obama's honesty about these struggles. Jason Marcil, a high school senior in New Hampshire, praises Obama for his candor. "I'm glad that he was honest about it," he said. "It's obvious that he's learned from his mistakes. He's been there. He knows what not to do."

Despite all these challenges, Barack Obama graduated from the Punahou School and was offered a full scholarship to a small, liberal arts college in California. Looking back on this period in his life, Obama has observed, "In no other country on earth is my story even possible."

COLLEGE AND SELF-DISCOVERY

> For about two years there, I was just painfully alone and really not focused on anything, except maybe thinking a lot.
>
> —BARACK OBAMA

Soon after graduating high school, Barack Obama enrolled at Occidental College, located in the Eagle Rock area just northeast of Los Angeles, California. Occidental was founded on April 20, 1887, by a group of Presbyterian clergy and laymen. The school's current campus, built in 1914, was designed by famed architect Myron Hunt. The college boasts a number of notable alumni including influential Christian philanthropist Howard Ahmanson Jr., former athlete and U.S. Senator Jack Kemp, actor Ben Affleck, and comic-book writer Dan Slott (best known for *Avengers: The Initiative* and *She-Hulk*). Occidental's campus architecture and its proximity to Hollywood have made it an ideal location for a number of film and television shoots, such as *Clueless, Star Trek III: The Search for Spock, Jurassic Park III, Orange County,* and the original *Beverly Hills 90210.*

As he settled into life at Oxy, Obama found a varied, decidedly international group of friends. On the campus of less than 2,000 students, Obama was surrounded by young Americans both white and black, as well as students from countries like France, India, Mexico, and Pakistan. Former classmates remember how Obama liked to watch L.A. Lakers basketball games and eat Indian food prepared by his friend Vinai Thummalapally.

In many ways Obama was just a normal kid, yet he impressed others with a self-assurance and brightness not readily seen in one so young. His global awareness grew as he learned from his coursework and peers, and he became very concerned about issues of both domestic and international politics. In an interview with the *LA Times*, Thummalapally remembers Obama saying at this time: "I want to get into political service. I want to write and help people who are disadvantaged." A summer trip to Pakistan with friends before his junior year cemented this desire within Obama, so stunned as he was by the poverty and economic disparity between classes in that country.

Although Obama would describe himself as "alienated" during his years at Occidental, his time there would ultimately set him on a course to public service. At college, he developed a sturdier sense of self and came to life politically, growing increasingly aware of harsh inequities like apartheid in South Africa and poverty in the third world.

Obama has made it extremely easy for all ages to get involved with the campaign. Young people are often intimidated by the size and grandeur of presidential campaigns and they feel there is no job for them. It has been truly inspiring to work with staff throughout the country, the vast majority of which is under 25, and see the enormous impact young people can make. Without the energy and determination of young staff members and volunteers, I do not think Barack Obama would be in the position he is today. The campaign has made it easy to feel that you are a part of the campaign, and I think this inspires young people to get involved so they can feel they were a part of history.

—AMY MCDONOUGH, COLLEGE STUDENT &
CO-CHAIR OF OCCIDENTAL COLLEGE STUDENTS FOR OBAMA

He also discovered that he wanted to be in a larger arena. In a *New York Times* article, one professor has described Occidental back then as feeling small and provincial, isolated from the rest of Los Angeles. Obama wrote in his memoir that he needed "a community that cut deeper than the common despair that black friends and I shared when reading the latest crime statistics, or the high fives I might exchange on a basketball court. A place where I could put down stakes and test my commitments."

In search of a place where he could deepen those commitments, Obama applied for a transfer program that Occidental had with New York City's Columbia University. He was accepted and, at age 20, headed to New York to pursue a degree in political science, focusing on international relations. Columbia is a member of the highly esteemed "Ivy League" of colleges. Founded as King's College in 1754, Columbia University is the oldest institution of higher education in the state of New York, and the sixth-oldest such institution in the United States. Its main campus lies in the Morningside Heights neighborhood of Manhattan.

Columbia has had a long association with U.S. political leaders. Four of the "founding fathers" of the United States were among the earliest students and trustees of the school. U.S. Presidents Theodore Roosevelt and Franklin D. Roosevelt studied law at Columbia. Dwight D. Eisenhower was president of the University before he was elected the 34th president of the United States. Poet, priest, and social activist Thomas Merton is an alumnus of Columbia, and converted to Catholicism while attending. Other celebrities of note who graduated from Columbia include actors Maggie Gyllenhaal, Julia Stiles, Amanda Peet, Famke Janssen, Matthew Fox, Jesse Bradford, and Ben Stein, as well as model Claire-Aimee Unabia.

College and Self-Discovery

At Columbia Obama made the decision to fully engage with his studies. He quit smoking marijuana. He continued running three miles a day, as he had done in California. He became involved with the Black Students Organization and participated in anti-apartheid activities. But life in New York City was not often easy for Obama. As a transfer student without much money, he lived in a series of dingy apartments all over New York—at least seven in the five years he spent in the city, from Upper West Side Manhattan to Brooklyn Heights to the Upper East Side. Sohale Siddiqi, a man with whom Obama shared an apartment for a while (referred to as "Sadik" in Obama's 1995 memoir), remembers the tiny places they lived with no real fondness. "It wasn't a comfortable existence. We were slumming it," Siddiqi told the Associated Press. They sat on furniture rescued from the streets, and listened to the sounds of gunfire at night.

As uncomfortable as his living situation may have been, it proved pivotal in Obama's later work. He writes of that time period, "It was only [then] that I began to grasp the almost mathematical precision with which America's race and class problems joined; the depth, the ferocity, of resulting tribal wars; the bile that flowed freely not just out on the streets but in the stalls of Columbia's bathrooms as well."

Obama's years in the alien metropolis of New York City are still not very well known or documented. He describes himself during this time as something of an academic monk, locked in the library and intently focused on his studies. Obama once confessed to a biographer, "For about two years there, I was just painfully alone and really not focused on anything, except maybe thinking a lot."

He also found solace in reading things beside his textbooks. "I did a lot of spiritual exploration," he has said of his time in New York. "I withdrew from the world in a fairly deliberate way." His exploration was aided by Saint Augustine, who wrote the world's first known spiritual memoir as a bishop in North Africa in the 4th century A.D. He also read 19th century German philosopher Friedrich Nietzsche and English fiction writer Graham Greene, a Catholic author whose novels are drenched in sadness, spiritual beauty, pain, and redemption. He spent a great deal of time wrestling with the words of these and other eminent authors.

On some restless Sundays Obama would wander into the back pews of church services in Harlem. "I'd just sit in the back and I'd listen to the choir and I'd listen to the sermon," he recalls of those lonely days. "There were times that I would just start tearing up listening to the choir and share that sense of release."

★ ★ ★ ★ ★

Looking back at this time in his life, Obama is certain he was searching out community, a place to belong. All the moving and school-changing and traveling he had experienced as a youth left him with, perhaps, a broader view of the world than most twentysomethings. But it also left him with an outsider's heart and a desire to be a part of something greater.

Obama began to explore the links between the African-American church and social movements of change. He devoured the works of Martin Luther King Jr. and other civil rights figures. His path was being shaped, though this is only entirely apparent in hindsight.

The years of transition from teenager to adult often warrant many hours gazing at walls and contemplating the existence of self and one's relation to the world. So, Obama too engaged in these willowy sessions of intense self-reflection. He knew where he had come from—what was he going to be and what did he believe?

Despite this self-imposed asceticism, Barack Obama's classmates remember him brightly. The president of MTV Networks, Michael J. Wolf, was in a seminar with Obama and remembers him as "very smart," adding, "He had a broad sense of international politics and international relations. It was a class with a lot of debate. He was a very, very active participant. I think he was truly distinctive from the other people in that class. He stood out."

The "stand-out" completed his undergraduate thesis on the topic of Soviet nuclear disarmament and graduated from Columbia in 1983. He remained in New York for another few years, regularly seeking out a position as a community organizer, but acquiescing to what he calls more "conventional" jobs to help pay off his many student loans. He worked for a couple of years as a writer for a business newsletter group that aided companies in understanding foreign markets. He spent a year as a coordinator for a nonprofit advocacy group at City College in Harlem, making a little less than $10,000 a year to promote government reform and environmental consumer advocacy among the students there.

Though he is remembered as something of a "rockstar associate" during his year at City College, Obama eventually became convinced it was going to be very difficult to work and live in the very expensive city of New York. In 1985 he made the decision to go to Chicago's South Side. It was there that his life and career ambitions began to fully take form.

THE COMMUNITY ORGANIZING EDUCATION

> Organizing teaches as nothing else does the beauty and strength of everyday people.

—BARACK OBAMA

Much has been made of Barack Obama's experience as a community organizer on the far South Side of Chicago in the mid-1980s. Some have dismissed this work as a rather trivial aspect of his résumé. For others, including Obama himself, his years with the Developing Communities Project (DCP) were both a foundational and pivotal part of his civic education. Ultimately, this experience has both led to and greatly influenced his historic run for the presidency of the United States.

After a few post-collegiate years in New York City, feeling frustrated by his career direction and the high cost of rent, Obama responded to a help-wanted ad put out by the Calumet Community Religious Conference (CCRC) in Chicago, seeking an individual to work with the mostly South Side churches involved in the Developing Communities Project, a spin-off of the CCRC. He met Gerald Kellman, one of CCRC's founders, for a job interview in a Manhattan coffee shop. After some intense questioning, Obama was hired on the spot. About a month later, he moved from New York to Chicago with the promise of a salary of about $10,000 a year, plus an extra $2,000 to buy a car to move to and get around in Chicago. He loaded all his belongings into a busted old Honda Civic to pursue a job that many others didn't quite understand.

Obama was often asked why an Ivy-league-educated young man with such great talents would want to spend his time working for a group of churches in inner-city Chicago for a small salary. "It needs to be done, and not enough folks are doing it," was his straightforward response to such questions. He'd seen *and lived* poverty, racism, and inequality, and he was determined to work for change at the most fundamental levels of community—beginning with individuals and the neighborhoods they live in.

Community organizing is an approach for developing power and relationships throughout local institutions such as congregations, unions, and associations. The U.S. civil rights movement, the anti-war movements, and the Chicano movement all influenced and were influenced by ideas of neighborhood organizing. Looking back at his time as a community organizer, Obama has said, "Community organizing is how ordinary people respond to out-of-touch politicians and their failed policies. Throughout our history, ordinary people have made good on America's promise by organizing for change from the bottom up."

Famous U.S. community organizers include Jane Addams, César Chávez, Martin Luther King Jr., John L. Lewis, Ralph Nader, and Paul Wellstone.

The Calumet Community Religious Conference was an organization designed to unite churches of the South Side and suburban Chicago area. The goal was to provide residents of these areas with a public voice and a strong collective power. Many of the people living in these sections of Chicago at the time had once been employed in the steel industry. Over the previous 20 years, the steel industry had declined and many factories were shut down. Jobs were lost and neighborhoods sunk deeper and deeper into poverty, becoming more vulnerable to crime, gang violence, and corruption. The majority of the residents of the South Side were African American, though there were also many whites and Latinos in these blue-collar neighborhoods.

At age 24, Obama was sometimes less than half the age of many of the people he was trying to organize, and he was the first to admit his inexperience with true grass-roots community development. But Obama was, by all accounts, a bright and confident (though self-effacing) man, open to learning and inviting those folks he met to learn right along with him.

He began by studying the renowned Alinsky method of community organization. Saul Alinsky was a social activist from Chicago who helped rally workers together during the Depression and for many years later. Alinsky's method focused on determining the self-interest and needs of individuals and acting to address those concerns, rather than pursuing some grand moral vision. Alinsky advocated a wide variety of strategies for applying pressure for political change, including some more confrontational tactics such as the picketing of official's homes. Obama rejected some of the more abrasive of Alinsky's tactics, but his coworkers from DCP point out he never had a problem with speaking truth to power honestly and directly.

However, taking the emphasis on self-interest to heart, Obama began his work for the newly created Developing Communities Project by going door-to-door to talk with people in their homes about the issues they most cared about. In a 1990 article published in the periodical *Illinois Issues*, Obama set forth these three primary characteristics of community organizing:

> Organizing begins with the premise that (1) the problems facing inner-city communities do not result from a lack of effective solutions, but from a lack of power to implement these solutions; (2) that the only way for communities to build long-term power is by organizing people and money around a common vision; and (3) that a viable organization can only be achieved if a broadly based indigenous leadership—and not one or two charismatic leaders—can knit together the diverse interests of their local institutions.

In contrast to conventional top-down change from government leaders, Obama learned that lasting change often rises organically from the bottom up—from the neighborhood, to the city, to the state, and even the nation. A member of the DCP board, Loretta Augustine-Herron, remembers Obama saying of organizing: "You've got to do it right; be open with the issues. Include the community instead of going behind the community's back... You've got to bring people together. If you exclude people, you're only weakening yourself. If you meet behind doors and make decisions for them, they'll never take ownership of the issue." Obama has carried this idea into his presidential campaign, offering each man, woman, and kid a chance to sing the song of change instead of *assuming* the tune and creating his own agenda.

Young Obama spent those years on the South Side bringing people together for the betterment of their communities. The work included long hours for little pay and was frequently frustrating. Every day was filled with at-risk youth to counsel, parks and playgrounds to be cleaned up, stop signs to install, and many other tasks and goals.

One day a resident at Altgeld Gardens, a geographically isolated public housing project surrounded by waste sites, brought a notice the residents had received about the planned removal of asbestos from the office of the housing project's manager. Obama organized the community to find out if there was asbestos in their apartments.

They persisted as officials lied and delayed, and then took a bus—with far fewer people than Obama had anticipated—to challenge authorities downtown. Ultimately, the city was forced to test all the apartments and eventually began cleaning them up. In his first book, *Dreams from My Father*, Obama writes that the bus trip changed him in a fundamental way, "because it hints at what might be possible and therefore spurs you on...That bus ride kept me going, I think. Maybe it still does."

★ ★ ★ ★ ★

Obama's work as a community organizer involved interaction with a wide range of churches and other religious groups. He found himself mobilizing congregations to work together with one another and sought to resolve rifts among churches of different denominations—the Protestant churches distrustful of the Catholic ones, and vice versa. Yet perhaps the most compelling part of his early years in Chicago before law school was his own decision to join a church and wholly practice the Christian faith.

Obama has said that his mother and grandparents were not particularly religious individuals, though they held sharp social concerns, high values, and a genuine love of people. In *The Audacity of Hope*, Obama discusses the spark that led him to consider and cherish the church:

> I was drawn to the power of the African-American religious tradition to spur social change...It had to serve as the center of the community's political, economic, and social as well as spiritual life; it understood in an intimate way the biblical call to feed the hungry and clothe the naked and challenge powers and principalities. I was able to see faith as more than just a comfort to the weary; rather, it was an active, palpable agent in the world.

During these first few years in Chicago, Obama was able to fully reconcile his own mother's teachings of loving all people and giving to those in need with the church for the very first time. In a recent speech to members of the African Methodist Episcopal Church, he affirmed that it was during this time that he "let Jesus Christ into my life," and added, "I dedicated myself to discovering his truth and carrying out his works."

In his three years at the DCP, he went from being a young hire to the director of the organization. Under his leadership the DCP grew to include a staff of thirteen and an annual budget of roughly $400,000. In a speech to the still-active DCP many years later, Obama spoke of growing up "to be a man, right here, in this area," mentioning further, "It's as a consequence of working with this organization and this community that I found my calling. There was something more than making money and getting a fancy degree. The measure of my life would be public service."

Obama felt profoundly the significance of his work, yet he longed to do more. During a visit to Kenya to meet the extended family he had never known, he learned of his father's unfortunate fate: His return to Kenya with a Harvard degree, his work as a high-ranking official in the government, and his eventual dissolution as his idealism faded and his frustration grew large. He learned that his father had eventually lost his job, and lived the remainder of his life impoverished.

It is clear that this news moved Obama. He knew for certain that he didn't want to end up in the same place as his father—woefully unhappy and too cynical to help. Thinking that perhaps the best way to ensure true change was to enter government, where he could enact legislation and synthesize all he'd already learned in Chicago, he decided he would leave his life as a community organizer and attend law school at his father's alma mater. Although he was leaving his job as a community organizer, Obama made a vow that he would come back to Chicago and reunite with those people and churches he had worked with so closely on the South Side—but this time from a different side of the power stratum.

Before leaving the DCP, Obama was meticulous in making sure that the transition to a new director would be smooth. Gerard Kellman, the man who had hired

> I would ask an undecided young voter what direction they want the country to go in over the next four years; do they want it to go in the same direction as the past eight years, or do they want to see change? I would ask them what kind of experience they want to see in the White House; do they want someone who has been sitting in Washington for several decades, or do they want someone with real experience working as a community organizer and solving many of the problems that Americans struggle with on a daily basis?
>
> —AMY MCDONOUGH, COLLEGE STUDENT & CO-CHAIR OF OCCIDENTAL COLLEGE STUDENTS FOR OBAMA

Obama after the single meeting in New York has said, "He took something that was really flimsy and built it into something strong." Thus, it seems both the DCP and Obama were the better for his three-year dedication and devotion to the nonprofit group and the community it aimed to help. Many times, Obama has said that his experience as an organizer was the best education he ever received—better even than the educations he received at both Columbia and Harvard. He puts it most wonderfully in that same article in *Illinois Issues*:

In return, organizing teaches as nothing else does the beauty and strength of everyday people. Through the songs of the church and the talk on the stoops, through the hundreds of individual stories of coming up from the South and finding any job that would pay, of raising families on threadbare budgets, of losing some children to drugs and watching others earn degrees and land jobs their parents could never aspire to—it is through these stories and songs of dashed hopes and powers of endurance, of ugliness and strife, subtlety and laughter, that organizers can shape a sense of community not only for others, but for themselves.

After a transient youth and an earnest search for identity, Obama had found a home—a community in which he developed deepened relationships, a church home, and a political identity. He honed his talent for listening, learned pragmatic strategies, practiced bringing varied people together, and developed a faith in ordinary citizens that still influences his campaign message. He discovered the importance of personal storytelling in politics and in faith communities.

It is known that during those years, Obama took consummate notes and created sketches of the varied strange and beautiful people he met, writing endearing short stories about some of them, though they have never been published. By the time he was ready to leave Chicago for Harvard, his old Honda Civic had finally given out, and Obama bought a little yellow Toyota Tercel for just $500. The car was all rust spots and floorboard holes, but it would take him back to the East Coast and the next chapter in his adult life.

BREAKING BARRIERS AT HARVARD LAW SCHOOL

That's what a Harvard education should buy—enough confidence and security to pursue your dreams and give something back.

—BARACK OBAMA

Barack Obama's time at Harvard Law School is generally one of the least-known stages of what has been a fascinating journey. In his book *Dreams from My Father,* Obama writes that he viewed law school as an avenue to give something back, to make a difference in people's lives. For him, it was a natural next step from the community and church work he had so loved in Chicago. By the time Obama received his law degree, he had his first national news media exposure, a book contract, and a shot of confidence that came from running the most powerful legal journal in the country. His time at Harvard also helped ground him in a collaborative process for reaching decisions, working with people from all sides of an issue.

Founded in 1636, Harvard is the oldest institution of higher learning in the United States. Harvard College was founded by the colony of Massachusetts with the goal of training ministers. An early brochure, published in 1643, declared the school's mission: "To advance Learning and perpetuate it to Posterity; dreading to leave an illiterate Ministry to the Churches." Harvard's early motto was "For Christ and the Church." A directive to its students laid out the purpose of all education: "Let every student be plainly instructed and consider well that the main end of his life and studies is to know God and Jesus, which is eternal life. And therefore to lay Christ at the bottom as the only foundation of all sound learning and knowledge."

Harvard Law School was established in 1817, making it the oldest continuously operating law school in the nation. It is home to the largest academic law library in the world and introduced back in 1870 what is now the standard first-year curriculum for all U.S. law schools—including classes in contracts, property, torts, criminal law, and civil procedure. Fourteen of the school's graduates have served on the U.S. Supreme Court, more than any other law school, and another four justices attended the school without graduating.

From the time he arrived in the fall of 1988, it was not an understatement to say that Obama seemed different than most of his fellow students. With his leather bomber jacket, big Afro, and worn-out jeans, 27-year-old Obama was both older and less stuffy than many of his classmates. He was one of only a very few African Americans among a group of students the Boston Globe described as "1,500 of America's most ambitious future lawyers, judges, and corporate executives." Financially, Harvard was a big stretch, and Obama went deep into debt with student loans to meet the $25,000-a-year cost. It was a huge commitment, but one that also offered Obama a measure of security, as he reflected in his book *The Audacity of Hope*: "One of the luxuries of going to Harvard Law School is it means you can take risks in your life. You can try to do things to improve society and still land on your feet. That's what a Harvard education should buy— enough confidence and security to pursue your dreams and give something back."

Obama lived all three years he spent at law school in a $700-a-month basement apartment in Somerville, Massachusetts, just north of Boston. A city of 77,478, Somerville is among the most densely populated areas of New England, with a working-class Irish American and Italian American population. From his landlord to the professors who mentored him, everyone seems to recall Obama as an exceptionally conscientious young man. But in some ways, he was just a typical, forgetful graduate student. Records from Somerville show that he still owes the city $72.63 in excise taxes and $45 in late penalties on two parking violations. As a law student Obama parked illegally in a bus stop in 1990 and illegally in a street-sweeping zone in 1991. Walter Pero, a Somerville city alderman, told the *Boston Globe* in 2007, "I kind of kidded with the mayor and said, 'If he [Obama] comes to Somerville, he might get booted.' "

While his age and appearance were unusual among his fellow students, what also set Obama apart from many of his classmates was his approach to analyzing an argument—the most critical skill in law school. Most young law students seek to demonstrate the merits of their beliefs through logic and determination, but Obama took a very different tack, preferring to listen, seek others' views, and find a middle way. "A lot of people at the time were just talking past each other, very committed to their opinions, their point of view, and not particularly interested in what other people had to say," Crystal Nix Hines, a former classmate who is now a television writer, told NBC News. "Barack transcended that."

★ ★ ★ ★ ★

It was this ability to overcome divisions and find common ground that motivated his fellow students to encourage Obama to seek to become an editor of the *Harvard Law Review*. The editors who worked on that journal were considered the most important group on campus. First published in 1887, the *Harvard Law Review* is known internationally as the most prestigious of all student-edited law reviews. At the end of his first year, Obama decided to apply for one of the 80 highly coveted positions on the law review. He nearly missed the deadline to apply when his beat-up 1984 Toyota Tercel broke down. But he made the deadline—and won a spot as an editor, based on his good grades and outstanding writing abilities.

In his second year, friends suggested Obama run to be the president of the law review, a position no African American had ever held. Initially, he did not want to apply, preferring to focus instead upon his goal of returning to Chicago as a community organizer. But Obama decided to run for law review president after a conversation with a fellow African-American friend, which he recounted in *Dreams from My Father*: "I said I was not planning to run and he said, 'Yes you are because that is a door that needs to be kicked down and you can take it down.'" Obama agreed to run for the job, saying he might be uniquely able to help heal the review's political and racial divisions.

The election was an intense, all-day event that seemed more like the reality TV show *Survivor* than anything else. The 19 contenders seeking to become president of the law review faced a board of peers that scrutinized their intellectual and social skills. *The Boston Globe* reported that the 61 editors not running for the job debated the merits of the candidates behind closed doors, while the hopefuls cooked them breakfast, lunch, and dinner. By midnight, the list of 19 candidates had been winnowed down to Obama and 24-year-old David Goldberg. A large conservative group of editors whose candidate had been defeated broke the standoff, pledging their support to Obama. "Whatever his politics, we felt he would give us a fair shake," said Bradford Berenson, a fellow Harvard student who went on to be an associate White House counsel in the Bush administration.

At about 12:30 a.m., the editors called Obama into the room, told him he had won, and broke into applause. Another editor pulled Obama in for a hug. "It was a hard hug, and it lasted a while," Obama told the school's newspaper, the *Harvard Law Record*. "At that point, I realized this was not just an individual thing...but something much bigger."

After he was elected, newspapers and magazines all across America swarmed Obama, the first black student to win the most coveted spot in the most vaunted club at one of America's most prestigious institutions. As a joke, a fellow student posted a cast list for a movie version of Obama's life, starring the popular Hollywood actor Blair Underwood. When Mr. Underwood visited the school later that year, he met with Obama, seeking material for his role on the popular TV show *L.A. Law*: "People were always asking me, do young black attorneys really exist like that?" Underwood said in a recent interview. "I would refer to Barack."

It is not surprising that winning the job proved much easier than actually doing it. In his new role, Obama had to review (and sometimes reject) articles by some of the school's famous professors. He also had to persuade a divided group of editors to stop arguing and start editing. Students who went on to work in the Supreme Court and the White House have said they never saw politics as bitter as at *Harvard Law Review* in the early '90s. Obama walked a delicate line, serving on the board of the Black Law Students Association, often speaking passionately about the controversy of the week, but in a way that white classmates say made them feel reassured rather than defensive. As much as he could, Obama stayed away from the extremes of campus debate, often choosing safe topics for his speeches. Obama spent long hours holed up in a second-floor office of Gannett House, a 19th-century building overlooking Cambridge Common.

In the spring of 1990, the campus was buzzing with arguments about affirmative action, which some students wanted to abolish. Affirmative action is the set of laws and regulations that seek to expand access to education or employment. These laws tend to help ethnic minorities, women, people with disabilities, and veterans. In an article on this period, the online site Slate reports that Obama listened to impassioned pleas from both sides, pressing both conservatives and liberals to sharpen their thinking. But despite the personal significance of the issue, Obama never offered his own point of view or discussed whether he believed he had benefited from affirmative action. "If anybody had walked by, they would have assumed he was a professor," Thomas J. Perrelli, a classmate who served as counsel to

Attorney General Janet Reno, told the *Boston Globe*. "He was leading the discussion but he wasn't trying to impose his own perspective on it. He was much more mediating."

Obama demonstrated this same skill in a very different place—on the basketball court. At Harvard Obama continued his passion of playing pickup basketball. Obama replaced his low-key off-court style with sharp elbows and aggressive grabs for the ball. The *Boston Globe* recounted a memorable game that revealed Obama's passion and calm on the court:

> It was just a five-on-five game between some law students at a Harvard gym, until someone jabbed a hard foul. An argument broke out, and pretty soon players were in one another's faces. To the players who were on the court that day, it seemed punches were about to be thrown. Then a skinny, soft-spoken forward with tight shorts and high socks named Barack Obama raced out from the sideline and put himself between two of the warring players.

One of Obama's friends from Harvard, Earl Martin Phalen, remembers Obama telling both teams, "Guys, this is not serious—it's just a pickup game." Looking back, Phelan commented, "There was all this testosterone exploding, and he just kind of had perspective...We ended up chilling it out."

It was also at Harvard that people got their first glimpse of Obama's extrordinary skills as a public speaker. Breaking with a long-held tradition, the Black Students Law Association asked him to deliver the keynote address at the group's annual conference in spring 1991. In a role that is typically reserved for legal scholars or tenured faculty, Obama gave a stirring speech. "It was a clarion call," Randall L. Kennedy, a law school professor who attended the conference, told the *Boston Globe*. "We've gotten this education, we've gotten this great halo, this great career-enhancing benefit. Let's not just feather our nests. Let's go forward and address the many ills that confront our society."

These days, Obama is seeking to end the warring in Washington with a warm message of unity and optimism. But years before he brought that message to the national political stage, he was defusing battles large and small from the sharp-elbowed basketball games to the cutthroat classrooms at Harvard Law School.

A LOVE STORY

She explained billable hours, and the rest was history...

—BARACK OBAMA

After his first year at Harvard Law School, Barack Obama returned home to Chicago for a summer job as an intern in a prestigious law firm. Sidney Austin is one of the oldest law firms in the world, and the sixth-largest U.S.-based corporate law firm—with over 1,800 lawyers, and offices in 16 cities worldwide.

On his first day at Sidney Austin, Obama met a striking young woman, Michelle Robinson, the lawyer assigned to be his summer advisor. In *The Audacity of Hope*, Obama wrote coyly about the day he met the woman who would one day become his wife:

> I remember that she was tall—almost my height in heels—and lovely, with a friendly, professional manner that matched her tailored suit and blouse.

She explained billable hours, and the rest was history—but not right away.

Michelle Obama remembers it a bit differently. She recalls that everybody at the firm was buzzing about the smart, first-year Harvard Law School student, so she was expecting to find him "nerdy, strange, off-putting" when they met. "But I was charmed," she told *Chicago* magazine. "I was pleasantly surprised by who he turned out to be."

Still, because of their professional relationship, Michelle Robinson got busy playing matchmaker, seeking to fix Obama up with her friends. Yet dating Michelle's friends was not exactly what an already smitten Barack Obama had in mind. Waiting for the right opportunity, halfway through the summer, Obama asked Michelle out.

"They were being careful—or she was," John Levi, the partner who hired them both, told the *Chicago Tribune*. "I gather she was reluctant to jump into an office romance." Michelle's brother Craig Robinson believes that's an understatement. In an interview with *Sports Illustrated* magazine, he said:

> You have to know a little bit about my father. My father was not college-educated, a hard-working man who raised two kids when he had multiple sclerosis, so the example we had was a father full of integrity, and that was the kind of guy my sister was looking

for. We used to joke as a family, "She'll never find a guy like that, because they don't exist anymore."

So when Michelle first brought Barack around that summer, Craig Robinson was convinced that Barack "was just another one who wasn't going to make it. Not that she had a lot of boyfriends, because she didn't; it was hard to pass muster with my sister. He had a gauntlet to go through."

But Michelle recognized that Barack's sense of purpose matched her own, and that was important as they met each other's friends—and each other's challenges. Before Michelle even agreed to go on a date with Obama, Craig Robinson recalls that, "she asked me to play basketball with him. Not to see [how good a] player he was, but because she'd grown up hearing my dad and I say you can tell a lot about a guy on the basketball court." Craig Robinson is not only Michelle's brother; he's the fourth-leading career scorer at Princeton University and is currently the head basketball coach at Oregon State. So what were the findings of his game with Barack? Michelle's big brother says plainly, "No personality flaws with respect to the basketball evaluation, so they started dating."

On their first date, Michelle and Barack saw Spike Lee's *Do the Right Thing*, appropriate for a couple who have each spoken of falling in love with the other's ideals. Their hearts and mutual desire for impactful change collided brilliantly. During the presidential campaign, Michelle told an audience about a night when she and Barack were courting:

He took me to a small church basement on the South Side of Chicago. He walked into that church basement just as comfortable and confident…and I knew he had been there before, and that this wasn't just a part-time fancy…and he talked about the simple notion that we as Americans understand the world as it is—and it is a world sometimes that is disappointing and unfair—but our job as American citizens is to work towards building the world as it should be. And as Barack spoke in that church basement, he moved me.

Having spent most of his life as an outsider with few firm roots and an often-divided family, Obama was immediately attracted to Michelle's circle of loving stability—her strong sense of family, her firm rooting in the community, and her deep Christian faith. "She wanted to be of service and he found that very attractive," recalls Gerald Kellman, who brought Obama to Chicago and trained him as an organizer.

★ ★ ★ ★ ★

Michelle Obama is a woman whose skills and accomplishments rival that of her accomplished husband. Her former community-organizing colleague Paul Schmitz told ABC News that Michelle "has a compass with as good a True North as anyone I've ever known. When she gives feedback, you *want* to follow it. She is a person driven to both discovering Truth, and fearless of expressing it—and honest feedback is one of the things Barack holds very valuable in their relationship."

Michelle described herself in a recent speech as a "little black girl from the South Side of Chicago, the daughter of working-class parents and the product of a public-school education." Her late father, Frasier Robinson, was a city pump operator and a Democratic precinct captain. Her mother, Marian, is a former Spiegel's department store secretary. Michelle was raised in a one-bedroom apartment on the top floor of a classic Chicago brick bungalow. Her mother still lives there, behind burglarproof wrought-iron doors and secured windows. In an interview with *Redbook* magazine, Michelle recalled how much she loved "girl stuff' when she was little. She set up an Easy Bake Oven in her bedroom. She sprawled across the carpet with the African-American versions of Barbie and her mate and their toy house and car. Later, as a young adult, children were "all she wanted," close friend and consultant Yvonne Davila told *Redbook*.

Michelle says she learned perseverance and hard work from her father, who continued to work for the Chicago water department even after he was diagnosed with multiple sclerosis:

My father taught me so much about work ethic. He was a blue collar city worker—worked his whole adult life at the water filtration plant on the South Side of Chicago. He got up, went to work every day, never complained, was never late. I knew he must have been frustrated with the physical restraints he had to contend with, as I never knew my father to walk without the assistance of a cane. But he also provided for our family. He did not go to college, but he was able to put two kids through Princeton on a single city worker salary—which is almost impossible today—and leave my mother a pension that now supports her.

Michelle Robinson and Barack Obama had dated for a couple of years, and she grew tired of hearing him question whether marriage still meant anything as an institution. So when Obama launched into another one of those discussions over dinner at a fancy restaurant in 1991, Robinson lit into her boyfriend, lecturing him on the need to get serious in their relationship. Then dessert came. On the plate was a box. Inside was an engagement ring. "He said, 'That kind of shuts you up, doesn't it?' " Michelle Obama recounted years later. The couple married the following year.

★ ★ ★ ★ ★

In 2007 Michelle and Barack Obama celebrated their 15th wedding anniversary at a place where they came together most intensely—their church. It was through Michelle that Obama found Chicago's Trinity United Church of Christ, where he was baptized. There, Obama studied the Bible with gifted teachers who he said would "gently poke me about my faith." With its commitment to social activism as a part of Christian life, the church was a good fit. "That community of faith suited me," Obama said in his autobiography. It was also a family place. Members refer to the sections in the massive sanctuary as neighborhoods; churchgoers go to the same neighborhood each Sunday and get to know the people who sit near them. They know when someone's sick or got a promotion at work.

Obama first met Jeremiah Wright, the church's sometimes-controversial pastor, while Obama was working as an organizer. They became friends, and after he married, Obama says, the two men would sometimes get together "after church to have chicken with the family—and we would have talked stories about our families." In his preaching, Wright often emphasized the importance of family, of staying married and taking good care of children. Obama's refrain that "responsibility does not end at conception" was inspired by countless conversations with Pastor Wright.

In an interview with *Christianity Today* magazine, Obama said this about his decision to accept Christ, "What was intellectual and what was emotional joined, and the belief in the redemptive power of Jesus Christ, that he died for our sins, that through him we could achieve eternal life—but also that, through good works we could find order and meaning here on Earth and transcend our limits and our flaws and our foibles—I found that powerful."

As young marrieds, Barack and Michelle (who also didn't go to church regularly as a child) went to church fairly often—two or three times a month. But after their first child, Malia, was born, they found making the effort more difficult. "I don't know if you've had the experience of taking young, squirming children to church, but it's not easy," Obama told the *Philadelphia Inquirer.* "Trinity was always packed, and so you had to get there early. And if you went to the morning service, you were looking at—it just was difficult. So that would cut back on our involvement."

Throughout his political career as a senator in Springfield and then Washington, Barack Obama has made an effort to make it home to Chicago most every weekend. Family life is a priority, which is why his family hasn't moved to Washington. "We made a good decision to stay in Chicago, so that has kept our family stable," Michelle once told a reporter for the *Chicago Tribune.* "There has been very little transition for me and the girls. Now he's commuting a lot, but he's the senator. He can handle it. That's really helped in keeping us grounded."

IN THE ILLINOIS STATE SENATE

> When he spoke on the floor of the Senate, he spoke out of conviction. You knew that—whether you agreed with him or disagreed with him.

> —CARL HAWKINSON, ILLINOIS STATE SENATOR (REPUBLICAN) FROM 1987-2003

The publicity that surrounded Barack Obama's election as the first black president of the *Harvard Law Review* led to a publishing contract for a book about race relations. After his graduation from Harvard Law School, the University of Chicago Law School provided Obama with a fellowship and an office to work on his book, in hopes of recruiting him to their faculty. In 1992, Obama began teaching Constitutional Law at the University of Chicago, something he continued to do for next 12 years.

From April to October of 1992, Obama directed Illinois' Project Vote, a voter registration drive with a paid staff of 10 and 700 volunteers. Project Vote registered 150,000 of the 400,000 unregistered African Americans in the state. *Crain's Chicago Business* magazine named Obama to its 1993 list of "40 under Forty" powers to be.

Obama originally planned to finish the book in one year, but it took much longer as the book evolved into a personal memoir. The manuscript was finally published in mid-1995 as *Dreams from My Father*. In an article about Obama for *Time*, columnist Joe Klein stated that the book "may be the best-written memoir ever produced by an American politician." Chicago author and lawyer Scott Turow also gave the writing high praise, suggesting that Obama's book "belongs on the shelf beside works like James McBride's *The Color of Water* and Gregory Howard Williams's *Life on the Color Line* as a tale of living astride America's racial categories."

In 1996, Obama ran for and was elected to a position on the Illinois Senate. He succeeded state Senator Alice Palmer as representative for Illinois' 13th District, which then spanned Chicago South Side neighborhoods from Hyde Park-Kenwood south to South Shore and west to Chicago Lawn. Although his experience as a community organizer and law professor served him well, Obama was a newcomer to elective politics, which allowed him to operate largely outside the city's Democratic machine.

Obama wrote that politics in the Illinois state capital were "a full-contact sport," and said he "minded neither the sharp elbows nor the occasional blind-side hit." Still in his thirties, Obama emerged as a leader by developing a style that former colleagues describe as methodical, inclusive, and pragmatic. He cobbled together legislation with Republicans and conservative Democrats, building bridges across ideological lines and making overtures other progressive politicians might have considered beneath them.

But Obama was not instantly embraced upon his arrival in the Illinois Senate. A fellow senator pointed out the fact that Obama was both a law professor (a *Constitutional-law* professor) and a Harvard graduate, causing many members of the General Assembly to roll their eyes.

Obama worked hard, and would often top off a long workday with a game of pickup basketball. He made the social rounds at Springfield parties, and joined a weekly card game with legislators and lobbyists in which the ante was only a dollar or two. One regular at these card games, former Democratic state Senator Larry Walsh, said Obama was competitive yet careful—and always hard to read. "One night, we were playing and things weren't going very well for me," Walsh recalled. "I had a real good hand and Barack beat me out with another one. I slammed down my cards and said, 'Doggone it, Barack, if you were a little more liberal in your card playing and a little more conservative in your politics, you and I would get along a lot better.' "

As he became more experienced in the Senate, Obama played an important role in drafting bipartisan legislation on issues of ethics and health-care reform, and overcame

Barack Obama's innovative political style has a unique appeal to the nation's youth. He seems to have the ability to combine genuine empathy, fighting passion, sharp intelligence, and a deep desire for change. In a nation where youth no longer trust a government they are highly disenchanted with, Barack Obama has given them hope.

MONICA TAYLOR, A VOLUNTEER TEACHER WITH R.E.A.L. BEAUTY SCHOOL, A PROGRAM SEEKING TO ENCOURAGE, EMPOWER, AND ENGAGE WITH TEENAGE GIRLS REGARDING ISSUES THEY FACE IN TODAY'S SOCIETY

law enforcement objections to codify changes designed to curb racial profiling. "When you come in, especially as a freshman, and work on something like ethics reform, it's not necessarily a way to endear yourself to some of the veteran members of the Illinois General Assembly," said state Sen. Kirk W. Dillard, a Republican who became a friend. "And working on issues like racial profiling was contentious, but Barack had a way both intellectually and in demeanor that defused skeptics."

"He wasn't a maverick," said Cynthia Canary, director of the Illinois Campaign for Political Reform. "There were other legislators I would turn to if I just wanted to make a lot of noise. That wasn't his style."

★★★★★

One of the most difficult pieces of legislation Obama worked on was a campaign finance effort, which came at the initiative of former U.S. Senator Paul Simon. A Republican and a Democrat in each legislative body were tapped to tighten a system that, among other things, allowed politicians to use campaign accounts for personal expenses. Obama was given the job of representing Senate Democrats by state Senator Emil Jones Jr. "He was very aggressive when he first came to the Senate," said Jones, now president of the state Senate. "We [Democrats] were in the minority, but he said, 'I'd like to work hard. Any tough assignments or things you'd like me to be involved in, don't hesitate to give it to me.' "

Obama favored more ambitious changes in campaign law, including limits on contributions, but adjusted the bill in search of consensus. "What impressed me about him was his ability in working with people of the opposite party," said Mike Lawrence, director of the Public Policy Institute at Southern Illinois University. "He had definite ideas about what ought to be contained in a campaign finance reform measure, but he also was willing to recognize that he was probably not going to get everything he wanted." The result, according to good-government groups, was the most ambitious campaign reform in nearly 25 years, making Illinois one of the best in the nation on campaign finance disclosure.

Obama also played a critical role in a complex debate that led to the 2003 reform of legislation regarding Illinois death penalty laws. In 2000, after the exoneration of a number of people who'd been sentenced to death, then-Governor George Ryan declared a moratorium on executions in the state until the state's policies and procedures could be reviewed. In proposing changes, Obama met repeatedly with officials and advocates on all sides. He nudged and cajoled colleagues fearful of being branded soft on crime, as well as death-penalty opponents worried that any reform would weaken efforts to abolish capital punishment.

Obama's signature effort was a push for mandatory taping of interrogations and confessions. It was opposed by prosecutors, police organizations, and Ryan's successor, Democrat Rod Blagojevich, who said it would impede investigators. Working under the belief that no innocent defendant should end up on death row and no guilty one should go free, Obama helped get the bill approved by the Senate on a 58 to 0 vote. When Blagojevich reversed his former position and signed it into law, Illinois became the first state to require taping of interrogations by statute. "Obviously, we didn't agree all the time, but he would always take suggestions when they were logical, and he was willing to listen to our point of view. And he offered his opinions in a lawyerly way," said Carl Hawkinson, the retired Republican chairman of the Judiciary Committee. "When he spoke on the floor of the Senate, he spoke out of conviction. You knew that, whether you agreed with him or disagreed with him."

Obama paid a dear political price for missing an important vote on a crime package during the 1999 Christmas holidays. When the legislature was called into special session to vote on gun control, Obama and his family were visiting his grandmother in Hawaii. His 18-month-old daughter, Malia, was sick and unable to fly. "I take my legislative responsibilities extremely seriously," Obama said after the measure fell five votes short. "I'm well aware of the potential risk of missing a vote, even if that vote doesn't wind up making the difference on a particular piece of legislation. But at some point, family has to come first." The measure was narrowly defeated, with Obama widely criticized for helping drive the loss.

That criticism may have played a part in the only electoral defeat of Obama's political career, which came when he sought to unseat U.S Representative Bobby Rush, a popular Chicago Democrat. Obama entered the race with the longtime U.S. Congressman in late September 1999, just six months before the primary. He told voters that Mr. Rush represented "a politics that is rooted in the past, a reactive politics that isn't good at coming up with concrete solutions." He promised new leadership, reaching beyond the black community and leading coalitions to take on contemporary problems, cut crime, expand health-care coverage, promote economic development, and expand educational opportunities. Obama lost by 31 points. Reflecting on this defeat in *The Audacity of Hope*, Obama wrote: "Less than halfway into the campaign, I knew in my bones that I was going to lose. Each morning from that point forward I awoke with a vague sense of dread, realizing that I would have to spend the day smiling and shaking hands and pretending that everything was going according to plan."

Obama returned to Springfield after this defeat, redoubling his efforts as a state senator. And he would return to the steps of Old State Capitol building in Springfield many times during his presidential campaign. He announced his candidacy there in February 2007. He announced his vice presidential running mate, Joe Biden, there in August 2008. Obama forged his political philosophy during his years as a state senator in Springfield, and he returns to Springfield often as a touchstone.

FAMILY LIFE AND FATHERHOOD

So I resolved many years ago that it was my obligation to break the cycle—that if I could be anything in life, I would be a good father to my girls.

—BARACK OBAMA

Like many other families, the Obamas have a tradition of going to church together on Father's Day. Barack and Michelle Obama have two daughters: Their first, Malia Ann, was born in 1998, followed by a second daughter, Natasha ("Sasha"), in 2001. During an interview with Jimmy Kimmel, Barack Obama was asked to describe a typical Father's Day at his house:

> We usually have some experiment with waffles or pancakes and there's a lot of cleanup afterwards...They come with stuff we wouldn't normally put on pancakes like whipped cream...Then we go to church.

Father's Day has great meaning for Obama, whose own father was a native Kenyan who had grown up herding goats. Obama's parents separated when he was two years old. His father eventually returned to Kenya and saw his son only once more before dying in an automobile accident in 1982. The younger Obama struggled with growing up without a father for much of his life.

Unfortunately, Obama's struggles are not unique. Since 1970, the U.S. Census reports the percentage of children living in mother-only families has more than doubled, increasing from 11 percent to 23 percent. More than half of the African-American children under 18 years old and nearly a third of Hispanic children in the United States live with only their mother, according to a 2006 Census Bureau report. This is a stark contrast to White and Asian families, where four out of five children under 18 live with both parents.

Social scientists have studied the impact of growing up without a father. The numbers are staggering:

- Children in father-absent homes are five times more likely to be poor. (Source: Horn, Wade F. Ph.D. and Tom Sylvester. 2002. "Father Facts Fourth Edition," National Fatherhood Initiative.)

- Children in father-absent families tend to score lower on standardized tests and to receive lower grades in school. (Source: Lynn M. Mulkey, Robert L. Crain.

2001. "One-Parent Households and Achievement: Economic and Behavioral Explanations of a Small Effect.")

- 70 percent of juveniles in state-operated institutions come from fatherless homes. (Source: U.S. Dept. of Justice, Special Report.)

- 80 percent of adolescents in psychiatric hospitals come from homes without a father. (Source: J.B. Elshtain, "Family Matters...," *Christian Century*, July 1993.)

- Children who exhibit violent misbehavior are 11 times as likely not to live with their fathers. (Source: (Sheline, Skipper, Broadhead, *American Journal of Public Health*, 1994.)

Visit any prison or spend time with any police officer and you will quickly learn that young men raised without a father in the home are significantly more likely to be engaged in criminal activity. In a 1998 study in *Behavioral Sciences & the Law*, University of South Florida Professor Kathleen M. Heide found that an astounding 72 percent of adolescents charged with murder grew up without their fathers. According to a 1990 article by Nicholas Davidson in *Policy Review*, 60 percent of men charged with rape grew up without their biological fathers. The United States is, in many ways, battling a silent epidemic, with children and mothers struggling to live without a father in the home.

In many ways, Barack Obama's story is a journey from fatherlessness to wholeness, as his best-selling book *Dreams from My Father: A Story of Race and Inheritance* points out. The book begins in New York, where Obama learns that his father—a figure he knows more as a myth than as a man—has been killed in a car accident. This sudden death inspires an emotional odyssey—first to a small town in Kansas, from which the younger Obama retraces the migration of his mother's family to Hawaii, and then to Kenya, where he meets the African side of his family, confronts the bitter truth of his father's life, and at last reconciles his divided inheritance.

You can see some of this journey and reconciliation in Obama's remarks during the summer of 2008 at Apostolic Church of God on Chicago's South Side. Obama urges the men gathered there to remember their responsibilities as fathers and be more engaged in raising their children. He tells of his own experience growing up without a father, and emphasizes that, of all the things he seeks to be in life, what he desires above all is to be a good father to his daughters. Obama's speech included these words:

> I know what it means to have an absent father, although my circumstances weren't as tough as they are for many young people today. Even though my father left us when I was two years old, and I only knew him from the letters he wrote and the stories

that my family told, I was luckier than most. I grew up in Hawaii, and had two wonderful grandparents from Kansas who poured everything they had into helping my mother raise my sister and me—who worked with her to teach us about love and respect and the obligations we have to one another. I screwed up more often than I should've, but I got plenty of second chances. And even though we didn't have a lot of money, scholarships gave me the opportunity to go to some of the best schools in the country. A lot of kids don't get these chances today. There is no margin for error in their lives. So my own story is different in that way.

Still, I know the toll that being a single parent took on my mother—how she struggled at times to pay bills; to give us the things that other kids had; to play all the roles that both parents are supposed to play. And I know the toll it took on me. So I resolved many years ago that it was my obligation to break the cycle—that if I could be anything in life, I would be a good father to my girls; that if I could give them anything, I would give them that rock—that foundation—on which to build their lives. And that would be the greatest gift I could offer.

Obama moves beyond his own personal story to speak to the broader issue of family and the role of fathers, particularly within the African-American community:

> Of all the rocks upon which we build our lives, we are reminded today that family is the most important. And we are called to recognize and honor how critical every father is to that foundation. They are teachers and coaches. They are mentors and role models. They are examples of success and the men who constantly push us toward it.
>
> But if we are honest with ourselves, we'll admit that what too many fathers also are is missing— missing from too many lives and too many homes. They have abandoned their responsibilities, acting like boys instead of men. And the foundations of our families are weaker because of it.
>
> You and I know how true this is in the African-American community. We know that more than half of all black children live in single-parent households, a number that has doubled—*doubled*—since we were children. We know the statistics—that children who grow up without a father are five times more likely to live in poverty and commit crime;

nine times more likely to drop out of schools and 0 times more likely to end up in prison. They are more likely to have behavioral problems, or run away from home, or become teenage parents themselves. And the foundations of our community are weaker because of it.

How many times in the last year has this city lost a child at the hands of another child? How many times have our hearts stopped in the middle of the night with the sound of a gunshot or a siren? How many teenagers have we seen hanging around on street corners when they should be sitting in a classroom? How many are sitting in prison when they should be working, or at least looking for a job? How many in this generation are we willing to lose to poverty or violence or addiction? How many?

In the early stage of his campaign for the Democratic nomination, Obama drew wild cheers in Beaumont, Texas, as he told a mostly African-American crowd that parents need to shape up, turn off the TV, help their kids with their homework, and stop letting them grow fat eating Popeye's chicken for breakfast. Some argued that he went too far in demonizing a particular group that is already struggling, while others praised him for pointing out what so many have been afraid to say. But whether they supported the speech or criticized it, interested voters have heard a call to higher expectations for fathers and for children. It's a call to empathy for others. Yes, this is a message from a politician, but it's more than that—it's a message that is thoroughly biblical and derived from Obama's own deep faith and personal experience.

Obama knows he is not a perfect father, but he has also made it clear that when he became a father he decided he would break the cycle and embrace his family. If their dad wins the presidency, Malia and Sasha Obama will be the youngest kids in the White House since Amy Carter. During this long election cycle, the girls have sometimes accompanied Obama on the campaign trail, occasionally bringing toys and water pistols along for fun. "It's a lot more fun than listening to Daddy talk," their mom once observed, prompting Sasha to raise her hands and open and close them as she said "blah, blah, blah," to mock her father talking. Obama knows his speeches don't always keep his daughters in rapt attention: "They basically cut out when I [start to speak]."

In his book *To Own a Dragon*, author Donald Miller encourages men who have experienced deep pain and loss created by a father's absence to see themselves as "wounded healers"—drawing on the pain they've experienced to offer solace and support to others. Barack Obama has done exactly that—taking his own experience of growing up without a father and turning it into a commitment to be a good dad to his own daughters. But the impact of this does not end with Malia and Sasha, nor with Obama's immediate family. By talking openly about his own struggles, Obama helps pave a path to empathy for millions of others who have grown up without their own fathers.

A BOLD ASSERTION

I don't oppose all wars. And I know that in this crowd today, there is no shortage of patriots, or of patriotism. What I am opposed to is a dumb war.

—BARACK OBAMA

One of the most well known of Obama's actions during his time as an Illinois state senator did not take place on the Senate floor in Springfield. On October 2, 2002, the same day President Bush and Congress agreed on a joint resolution authorizing the war on Iraq, Obama addressed an anti-war rally at Federal Plaza in Chicago. Although the decision to go to war in Iraq has been roundly debated and criticized in more recent years, at the time, Obama was one of a very select few political leaders who spoke out against the war.

The U.S. war in Afghanistan had begun a year earlier, on October 7, 2001. That war was launched by the

United States and the United Kingdom in response to the September 11, 2001, attacks on America. Many saw this battle in Afghanistan as the beginning of a global war on terror. By fall of 2002, the U.S. Congress was debating a resolution authorizing the use of military force against Iraq, a measure that had the support of large bipartisan majorities. The resolution authorized President Bush to use the Armed Forces of the United States "as he determines to be necessary and appropriate" in order to "defend the national security of the United States against the continuing threat posed by Iraq; and enforce all relevant United Nations Security Council Resolutions regarding Iraq."

In the United States, there were limited demonstrations against the proposed war on Iraq mainly organized by anti-war organizations that had formed in opposition to the invasion of Afghanistan. Over 100,000 people took part in a protest in Washington and more than 50,000 people took part in a demonstration in San Francisco. These demonstrations tended to be predominately young people, many of whom were attending the first formal protests of their lives. Europe saw the biggest number of protesters, including a rally of 3 million people in Rome, which is listed in the *Guinness Book of Records* as the largest ever anti-war rally.

Barack Obama's opposition to the Iraq War was influenced a great deal by his study of Dr. Martin Luther King Jr.'s opposition to the war in Vietnam. As early as

1965, King began to express publicly his doubts about the role of the United States in the Vietnam War. On April 4, 1967—exactly one year before his death—King delivered a speech titled "Beyond Vietnam" from the pulpit of New York City's Riverside Church. In the speech, King spoke strongly against the U.S. role in the war, stating that the United States was in Vietnam "to occupy it as an American colony." In what many saw as the most controversial portion of his speech, King called the U.S. government "the greatest purveyor of violence in the world today." He declared that the country and its leaders needed a moral overhaul:

> A true revolution of values will soon look uneasily on the glaring contrast of poverty and wealth. With righteous indignation, it will look across the seas and see individual capitalists of the West investing huge sums of money in Asia, Africa, and South America, only to take the profits out with no concern for the social betterment of the countries, and say: "This is not just."

King also opposed the Vietnam War because it took money and resources that could otherwise have been dedicated to the War on Poverty. He bluntly stated the moral ramifications of our nation's continuing to devote more and more money to war and less and less to ending poverty: "A nation that continues year after year to spend

I support Barack Obama for countless reasons, but one of the most important is his stance on the Iraq War. The fact that he was able to foresee the failure of the war and speak out against it when everyone else was silent shows a great deal about his character and determination. I also feel his diplomatic approach to dealing with foreign countries is the kind of foreign policy we need. I would much rather see the next U.S. president sit down with the leaders of Iran and attempt some sort of peaceful reconciliation.

—AMY MCDONOUGH, COLLEGE STUDENT & CO-CHAIR OF OCCIDENTAL COLLEGE STUDENTS FOR OBAMA

more money on military defense than on programs of social uplift is approaching spiritual death."

Obama spoke before a crowd of about 1,000 gathered at Federal Plaza in Chicago in October 2002. That crowd included college students, middle-aged people concerned about the Iraq War, and older people who had protested against the Vietnam War 40 years before. This rally was the first public effort in Chicago that spoke out against the Bush administration's plan for war in Iraq. The opposition to this war had just begun to take hold in the city that many see as the capital of the heartland of America. "I've been surprised in the last three or four weeks how vocal people have become against war in Iraq," Rev. Paul H. Rutgers, executive director of the Council of Religious Leaders of Metropolitan Chicago, told a newspaper at the time. One of the rally organizers, Jennifer Amdur Spitz, emphasized the broad base of support for the protest: "It's not coming from above," she told a local TV reporter. "It's coming from across all generations, all walks of life. This is not a fringe movement."

Among the college students in the crowd was Amanda Klonsky, 23, whose father was a member of Students for a Democratic Society, a protest group from the 1960s. Klonsky told a local reporter at the 2002 Chicago rally:

> This one, the impending Iraq war, really began to scare me. The people who are in Washington right now scare the pants off me. I think it's the most dangerous administration not just in my lifetime, but possibly the entire American century. Whatever I can do, I'll do, even though it seems like little more than punching a keyboard.

The Rev. Jesse Jackson took to the podium first at the Chicago protest. Jackson is a Chicago-based civil rights activist and Baptist minister, who was a candidate for the Democratic presidential nomination in 1984 and 1988. In 1965, Jackson had participated in the Selma to Montgomery marches organized by King and other civil rights leaders in Alabama, and he later was selected by King to lead the Chicago chapter of the Southern Christian Leadership Conference (SCLC).

In his article about the rally, Frank James of the *Chicago Tribune* recalled Jackson's words to the gathered audience: "This is a rally to stop a war from occurring," Jackson said. Then he implored the crowd to look to the sky and count to 10. "I just diverted your attention away from the rally. That's what George Bush is doing. The sky is not falling and we're not threatened by Saddam Hussein."

Obama followed Jackson at the podium. Although Obama had been a supporter of the 2001 war in Afghanistan, he had grave misgivings about the U.S. plan for a pre-emptive war in Iraq. Working from conversations with colleagues on all sides of the issue, he had assembled his thoughts on sheets of yellow legal paper. Looking out at the group of chilly protestors, he spoke these words:

> My grandfather signed up for a war the day after
> Pearl Harbor was bombed, fought in Patton's army.
> He saw the dead and dying across the fields of Eu-

rope; he heard the stories of fellow troops who first entered Auschwitz and Treblinka. He fought in the name of a larger freedom, part of that arsenal of democracy that triumphed over evil, and he did not fight in vain.

I don't oppose all wars.

After September 11th, after witnessing the carnage and destruction, the dust and the tears, I supported this Administration's pledge to hunt down and root out those who would slaughter innocents in the name of intolerance, and I would willingly take up arms myself to prevent such a tragedy from happening again.

I don't oppose all wars. And I know that in this crowd today, there is no shortage of patriots, or of patriotism. What I am opposed to is a dumb war. What I am opposed to is a rash war. What I am opposed to is the cynical attempt by Richard Perle and Paul Wolfowitz and other armchair, weekend warriors in this Administration to shove their own ideological agendas down our throats, irrespective of the costs in lives lost and in hardships borne.

What I am opposed to is the attempt by political hacks like Karl Rove to distract us from a rise in the uninsured, a rise in the poverty rate, a drop in the median income—to distract us from corporate scandals and a stock market that has just gone through the worst month since the Great Depression.

That's what I'm opposed to. A dumb war. A rash war. A war based not on reason but on passion, not on principle but on politics.

What Obama characterized as a "dumb war" had motivated first-time protestors like Ayne Dowd, 21, of Omaha, who attended the rally with three of her classmates at DePaul University in Chicago. "It's very cool, very empowering," Dowd told a local newspaper. "I think this can grow," said Andrea Juracek, another young protester. "More people are against the war rather than for it. When the word gets out, people will start coming out."

Obama drew on portions of Dr. King's speech "Beyond Vietnam" as he went on to say:

Now let me be clear—I suffer no illusions about Saddam Hussein. He is a brutal man. A ruthless man. A man who butchers his own people to secure his own power. He has repeatedly defied U.N. resolutions, thwarted U.N. inspection teams, developed chemical and biological weapons, and coveted nuclear capacity. He's a bad guy. The world, and the Iraqi people, would be better off without him.

But I also know that Saddam poses no imminent and direct threat to the United States, or to his neighbors, that the Iraqi economy is in shambles, that the Iraqi military a fraction of its former strength, and that in concert with the international community he can be contained until, in the way of all petty dictators, he falls away into the dustbin of history.

I know that even a successful war against Iraq will require a U.S. occupation of undetermined length, at undetermined cost, with undetermined consequences. I know that an invasion of Iraq without a clear rationale and without strong international support will only fan the flames of the Middle East, and encourage the worst, rather than best, impulses of the Arab world, and strengthen the recruitment arm of al-Qaeda.

I am not opposed to all wars. I'm opposed to dumb wars.

> The war in Iraq is one of my biggest concerns. I have friends and neighbors who are serving in Iraq. When Obama spoke out against the war, he did not sound like a politician talking like one. He made me think he was opposed to the war, but I liked his thoughtful approach. He seemed much more comfortable with things that are complex, rather than quick sound bites.
>
> —NICOLE DEANE, A FRESHMAN AT UNIVERSITY OF SOUTHERN CALIFORNIA

At the time, Obama's speech received little attention in the local or national press. The headline news of that day was the U.S. Senate's voting 77-23 to authorize President Bush to attack Iraq if Saddam Hussein refused to give up weapons of mass destruction as required by U.N. resolutions. Hours earlier, the House approved an identical resolution, 296-133. The president praised the congressional action, declaring, "America speaks with one voice." Yet it's clear that Obama's was one of many voices with divergent opinions that were not being heard.

Although the speech received relatively little attention at the time, it put Obama on record as an early opponent of the Bush administration's policies on Iraq. Many of the supporters of Obama's improbable run for presidency have quoted from this 2002 speech decrying the attack on Iraq, noting that it predicts many of the failures that eventually came to pass. Obama's speech also provides an insight into the "third way" approach that has defined Obama, forging a path that was neither liberal nor conservative—opposing the Iraq War while still supporting war as a tactic for the U.S.

It would not be long before Obama would have the chance to express his views on an even larger playing field.

THE YEAR EVERYTHING CHANGED

Maybe it was almost like magic, because it was one of those things that happened exactly right.

—JIM CAULEY

When news arrived in April 2003 that the incumbent U.S. Senator from Illinois, Republican Peter Fitzgerald, would not run for re-election in 2004, there was a mad rush among politicians vying to fill his open seat, especially among those in the Democratic Party. At that time both houses of the U.S. Congress held a Republican majority. George W. Bush was wrapping up his first term as president, and the Iraq War had just begun. Many were unhappy with the state of the country, and growing unhappier about the war in the Middle East.

Barack Obama was still a state senator at the time, and after some deliberation, decided to throw his name into the Democratic primary race for a chance in the general election. Obama could hardly have known then that he was embarking on a path that would shatter many precedents and end in a historical, almost magical manner.

Obama was one of seven Democratic candidates (joining eight Republicans) competing in their respective primaries in an effort to claim Fitzgerald's seat in the Senate. Together, these candidates spent $60 million—the Democrats alone spent an unheard of $46 million—making it the most expensive U.S. Senate primary in election history. After leading contender, Democrat Blair Hull, became mired in a domestic abuse scandal, Obama surged ahead in the polls and won the March 2004 primary with an incredible margin of 29 percent over runner-up, Dan Hynes.

Polls soon after the primaries suggested that Obama held a lead of at least 22 points over Jack Ryan, the man determined to be his Republican rival in the general election. However, scandal again caused his opponent to step out of the race. Ryan had been married to Hollywood actress Jeri Ryan in the '90s, during which they had one child before divorcing in 1999. During Ryan's primary run and afterward, several groups including the *Chicago Tribune* newspaper, the Chicago ABC-affiliate television station, and other GOP rivals petitioned a Los Angeles judge to release records from the court proceedings during the divorce and custody hearings. Eventually, all the records were released, and Jeri Ryan's claims of her ex-husband's sordid sexual behavior wreaked irreparable havoc on Ryan's campaign. He withdrew from the race in late June, and Obama remained unopposed as a candidate for many weeks following.

The withdrawal of the Republican candidate, coupled with Obama's already substantial lead, allowed Obama to relax his campaign a bit. He was soon stumping for fellow Democrats outside of Illinois, building a strong network of allies. In the 2004 presidential elections, the Democrats had chosen Massachusetts Senator John Kerry as the candidate they hoped would defeat President Bush in his bid for a second term in office. Obama's advisors began exhaustively lobbying Kerry's campaign, offering to help, and asking for a [long]shot to speak at the 2004 Democratic National Convention (DNC) to be held in Boston during the last week of July.

Nobody in Washington knew just what to make of this charismatic young politician who seemed to have arisen out of nowhere. The man who organized the DNC for Kerry's campaign was Jack Corrigan, who told the *Washington Post* there were some concerns about inviting Obama to speak: "The hesitation on him as a speaker was that he didn't even hold federal office yet, so how prominent could he be?" adding, "He was unproven. But we became convinced that he also offered incredible promise."

After some deliberation the Kerry campaign called Obama to offer him the opportunity to make the keynote speech. He accepted, and got to work that same day on a first draft of the speech, which he wrote out by hand on a legal notepad. Though advisors had penned speeches for him from time to time during his political career, Obama was fiercely determined to write this one on his own. He knew others wouldn't wholly react if his words weren't truly out of his own head and heart. Jim Cauley, his Senate campaign manager has said of the now famous speech: "He wanted everything to be in his own words. He guarded it. He made it clear from the beginning that this speech was going to be his baby."

Over the course of the next weeks, Obama—who always loved writing—often escaped to the restroom to find a quiet space to compose alone. He also reportedly spent a great deal of time going over video and speeches of conventions from the previous 30 years. He'd always been meticulous, and in the heat of the spotlight—he felt he had to get this right.

After weeks of diligent work, Obama had a speech that would run about 25 minutes—far longer than the 12 minutes the DNC had allotted. Initially, the DNC refused to budge on the time constraint. So Obama worked with some senior advisors to cut his speech down and ended up with something closer to 17 minutes. The DNC took the compromise.

Before Obama boarded the plane for Boston, he rehearsed the speech nearly 30 times. Someone tracked down a teleprompter for him to practice with, since he'd never used one before. At first, the words fell from his mouth stilted and awkward. But as Obama practiced and memorized the sentences he'd written—words that told his own American story—the sharp edges softened a bit.

As Barack and Michelle flew by chartered plane to Boston, Obama mused on his experience four years earlier at the 2000 Democratic convention—by all accounts a fiasco. He had taken a last-minute budget flight from Chicago to Los Angeles. When he arrived at the airport, his credit card was rejected by a rental car company. When he finally reached the arena where the event was being held, he wasn't even allowed in the doors and had to watch much of the convention on a Jumbotron outside.

Four years later, things were shaping up very differently. Obama was getting ready to deliver what he already sensed would be the most important speech of his life. He'd done a great amount of preparation work before leaving Illinois, but he was still anxious and restless. The day before he was to speak, Obama sought out Kevin Lampe, an old friend of his who was working at the convention, and requested two favors: First, that Michelle would be allowed backstage with him before, during, and after his address to the delegates. (Friends and family were rarely allowed in that space.) Second, that he might be allowed an extra rehearsal. Speakers typically only got two chances to prepare in the space with the teleprompter and all. He was granted both wishes.

Those who attended Obama's rehearsals recall thinking he was still a bit off. Despite the extra practice and the input of a speech coach, he didn't seem to be improving. Illinois Senator Richard Durbin, who introduced Obama that night, later reflected:

> You've got to try to picture this, the atmosphere, the pressure that comes with standing by yourself in front of all those people. One minute you're backstage, and then someone pushes you out there, and suddenly you're smack dab in the center of the spotlight…I think it's probably the hardest assignment you can have.

★ ★ ★ ★ ★

The day of his keynote address, Obama spent most of the morning in interviews and meetings. That night, last-minute costume changes put him in someone's borrowed blue tie. He stood backstage with his wife and listened to Senator Durbin's introduction, steeling himself for the moment. When his time to walk out finally arrived, he strode confidently out to the podium, this handsome,

42-year-old biracial American who was, even then, still virtually unknown to the greater public. He wasn't even a national politician yet—that wouldn't come for another few months.

He began a bit shakily. The teleprompter was cutting off words, his nerves stormed. Humbly, he announced: "Tonight is a particular honor for me because, let's face it, my presence on this stage is pretty unlikely." When his mention of his mother's birthplace brought a spontaneous cheer from the Kansas delegates, he beamed and waved, graciously, unscripted. Those who knew him well could see his shoulders relax as he grew suddenly comfortable and launched into his story with a keen and careful momentum.

Long ago, while working as a community organizer, he had learned the importance of sharing one's story with people, of the transformative power it can hold.

And now Obama shared his own story with both the delegates in the arena and the folks watching or listening at home: "I stand here knowing that my story is part of the larger American story, that I owe a debt to all of those who came before me, and that, in no other country on earth, is my story even possible." He emphasized the unique hope that America offered as a country and the beautiful complexities of the American people.

Obama took time to promote Senator Kerry's credentials, and mentioned the conflict of war, as well as the responsibility of the government to those citizens it sends to fight:

> When we send our young men and women into harm's way, we have a solemn obligation not to fudge the numbers or shade the truth about why they're going, to care for their families while they're gone, to tend to the soldiers upon their return, and to never ever go to war without enough troops to win the war, secure the peace, and earn the respect of the world.

Applying lessons taught to him in early childhood by his mother, later reinforced by his work on Chicago's South Side, he asked Americans to recognize not how they are different from one another, but all a part of the same great community—a community of people who, echoing New Testament teachings, have an obligation to take care of one another:

> For alongside our famous individualism, there's another ingredient in the American saga, a belief that we're all connected as one people. If there is a child on the South Side of Chicago who can't read, that matters to me, even if it's not my child. If there is a senior citizen somewhere who can't pay for their prescription drugs, and having to choose between medicine and the rent, that makes my life poorer,

even if it's not my grandparent. If there's an Arab American family being rounded up without benefit of an attorney or due process, that threatens my civil liberties. It is that fundamental belief—I am my brother's keeper, I am my sister's keeper—that makes this country work. It's what allows us to pursue our individual dreams and yet still come together as a single American family.

Nearing the end of his 17 minutes, Obama's address began escalating to a fever pitch, calling for a recognition of the many things Americans hold in common, shattering partisan myths of the Red States and the Blue States, and asking the question that has become so key to the entirety of his political career: "Do we participate in a politics of cynicism or do we participate in a politics of hope?" He went on to boldly declare: "I believe that we have a righteous wind at our backs and that as we stand on the crossroads of history, we can make the right choices, and meet the challenges that face us," before ending poignantly, with that same note of hope, "And out of this long political darkness a brighter day will come."

Friend and state Senator Terry Link, who was watching from the stands, confesses that at the conclusion of the speech, "I was feeling like a proud older brother, and I had tears coming out of my eyes when he finished." He adds, "Wanting to be a tough guy, I was wiping tears on the corner of my suit coat and trying to clean up. Then I turn around and see there's not a dry eye in the whole place. He got to everybody." Cauley offers of the night, "Maybe it was almost like magic, because it was one of those things that happened exactly right."

Whatever it was, Obama soared to political superstardom in those several minutes. His story, his words, his charisma connected with people and led them to believe that it was possible to once again choose the politics of hope over fear and cynicism.

Obama's life was unavoidably and permanently altered from the minute he stepped off that stage in Boston. In the hours and days to come, it would become apparent that his quiet private life would be greatly diminished as a result. People fought for his time. Security had to be hired. Crowds had to be managed. And he *still* was not yet even a U.S. senator—the elections were still three months away.

Several days after Obama's life-changing address to the Democratic National Convention, an African-American Republican named Alan Keyes announced he would be running for the seat in the November general election against Obama. Thus, one more historic milestone was reached when Obama and Keyes became the first two African-American contenders to represent the major parties in a U.S. Senate race.

Alan Keyes had run for senator twice before—in Maryland, but had lost both tries. He was also an early Republican presidential candidate in the elections of 1996 and 2000. Keyes had relocated to Illinois just days before announcing his candidacy, and was considered by some to be a "carpetbagger" (a pejorative term for one who moves to another state for the sake of political expediency). But Obama welcomed him to the race, accepting the challenge he presented: "Illinoisans want a Senate candidate who will attack the problems they and their families face rather than spending time attacking each other. I invite him to join me in such a race."

There were six tooth-and-nail debates between the two, but on Election Day, November 2, 2004, the Illinois Senate race was one of the first to be called—in Barack Obama's favor. He won by a landslide, carrying about 70 percent of the votes to Keyes' 27 percent. The margin of victory was the largest in the history of U.S. Senate contests in Illinois—just one more "first" in what has been often called a fairy-tale year for Obama.

A U.S. SENATOR PAVES THE WAY

As the individual hopelessly mars himself if he lets his conscience be dulled by the constant repetition of unworthy acts, so the nation will hopelessly blunt the popular conscience if it permits its public men continually to do acts which the nation in its heart of hearts knows are acts which cast discredit upon our whole public life.

—BARACK OBAMA

When Barack Obama took his oath as U.S. senator for Illinois in January of 2005, he became only the third African American to join the Senate since Reconstruction. In 1966, Republican Edward William Brooke III of Massachusetts became the first African American to be elected to the U.S. Senate by popular vote. In 1993, Carol Mosley Braun, a Democrat from Chicago, became the first African-American woman as well as the first African-American Democrat to serve in the U.S. Senate.

Despite the historic nature of his election, Obama was merely a freshman senator, considered raw and naive by many elder legislators. For the first two years of his term, he was 99th in seniority (of 100 colleagues) and, as a Democrat, was a member of the minority party, since Republicans held a majority of the seats. At 43, he was markedly younger than most of his colleagues—the average age of the Senators in the 109th Congress was 60 years old.

By all accounts, Obama kept a low profile his first year serving in Congress, but his actions were deliberate and methodical. He met with elder, distinguished statesmen—seeking their advice and cooperation. He became a true student of the Senate, attempting to learn all the ins and outs of crafting legislation and debating it on the Senate floor. Slowly, he gained the admiration of those with many more years of experience and became friends with the esteemed Senator Ted Kennedy of Massachusetts and others.

The details of policy and law, resolutions and co-sponsorships, can seem tricky and even dull at first. But taken as a whole, the efforts a senator makes, the legislation drafted and committees joined, paint a remarkable picture of what he or she cares most ardently about. Obama is no different. By exploring his work in nearly four years of his term, one may trace the patterns of his passions and pull more ribbons from the larger story of his life and labors.

The Senate has 20 specialized committees and many more subcommittees to enable more comprehensive consideration of various pieces of legislation. Obama serves on four of these committees, and his choices reflect the areas of public policy he most cares about. He is a member of the Foreign Relations (chaired by vice presidential candidate Joe Biden); Veterans Affairs; Health, Education, Labor and Pensions (HELP); and Homeland Security and Governmental Affairs committees. A great number of the bills authored, introduced, and cosponsored by Senator Obama revolve around the issues focused upon by these groups. A review of his work in the Senate underscores what Obama put into law to better our communities, the country, and the world as a whole.

★ ★ ★ ★ ★

The first bill Obama introduced as a U.S. senator was the Higher Education Opportunity Through Pell Grant Expansion Act (HOPE), which would increase the maximum Pell Grant award from $4,050 to $5,100, helping more U.S. students afford a college education. While many if not most political officials come from more economically privileged backgrounds, Obama had to take out many student loans as part of his own schooling, so he is more personally aware than most Senators of the high cost of quality secondary education. The scope of the Pell Grant program is enormous, touching millions of students over its more than 40-year history. In 2005-06, the program covered one-third of the yearly cost of higher education at a public four-year institution in the United States.

Obama also supported a boost for the Head Start program, which helps engage young children in school from the very beginnings of their educations. Created in 1965, Head Start is the longest-running program to address systemic poverty in the United States. As of late 2005, more than 22 million preschool-aged children have participated in Head Start. Obama's concerns also span literacy and the desire to train and maintain exceptional teacher presence in the classroom. Education is a passion that Obama learned from his mother and maternal grandparents.

Concerning crime, Obama cosponsored Dru's Law, which created a nationwide sex offender database and requires the monitoring of sexual offenders upon leaving prison. He also cosponsored the Sex Offender Regulation and Notification Act, a law that increased the penalties for sex offenders accused of crimes involving children under age 12.

Obama also cosponsored the reauthorization of the Violence Against Women Act, passed in October 2005. Originally authored by Joe Biden, this act provided funding to enhance investigation and prosecution of violent crimes perpetrated against women, increased pre-trial detention of the accused, provided for automatic and mandatory restitution by those convicted, and allowed civil redress in cases prosecutors choose to leave unprosecuted. In a speech given in Washington DC the same year, Obama articulated his commitment to aiding women and women's rights:

> From the first moment a woman dared to speak that hope—dared to believe that the American Dream was meant for her too—ordinary women have taken on extraordinary odds to give their daughters the chance for something else; for a life more equal, more free, and filled with more opportunity than they ever had. In so many ways we have succeeded, but in so many areas we have much work left to do.

As the son of a single mother, as a brother and a husband, and as father of two young girls, Obama has a passionate and profoundly personal interest in the concerns of women in America today. The measures he has supported to lift women out of situations of violence and domestic · abuse are just one way he has expressed his commitment to helping women move toward true equality.

Obama's Senate career has also shown a marked interest in the issues of energy and the environment. He authored the Fuel Economy Reform Act, designed to raise fuel efficiency standards ("CAFE") in automobiles, and also introduced the American Fuels Act, seeking to increase the use of biofuels over conventional nonrenewable fuels. Obama has recognized, and berated, the larger political bodies for their lack of resolution on the issue of climate change. In a speech given in 2006, he spoke passionately about this problem:

> And yet, when it comes to finding a way to end our dependence on fossil fuels, the greatest vacuum in leadership, the biggest failure of imagination, and the most stubborn refusal to admit the need for change is coming from the very people who are running the country.

Senator Obama recognizes that the need to care for our earth spans both global and local issues. Returning to his community organizer roots, he introduced the Healthy

> I say that the very fact that the excitement that surrounds him speaks to his transcending partisan gridlock. There is a sort of transcendence about his political ideology.
>
> —ALEXANDER STEVENS, COLLEGE STUDENT

Communities and Healthy Places Acts, working to remove unsafe chemicals and other products from neighborhoods and building projects. Another significant endeavor culminated in the Lead Toy Act, which restricted the sale, distribution, and transportation of lead-based toys.

Ethics and lobbying reform is another area in which Obama has been extremely influential. The Legislative Transparency Act introduced comprehensive reforms in the areas of ethics and lobbying. This act, which passed by a huge majority and was signed into law in September 2007, drew heavily from a bill authored by Obama and Republican Senator Russ Feingold. It included bans on gifts to legislators from lobbyists, and the disclosure of contributions that lobbyists collect for candidates, party committees, etc.—a provision widely regarded as "sweeping" reform and likely to have huge positive impact on Washington. Obama frequently works across party lines for the issue he cares about, knowing all too well that reform must be made on both sides of the aisle.

Barack Obama also helped author the Honest Leadership and Open Government Act, which strengthens public disclosure requirements concerning lobbying activity and funding, places more restrictions on gifts for members of Congress and their staff, and provides for mandatory disclosure of earmarks in expenditure bills. In a speech at a Lobbying Reform Summit in 2006, Obama addressed the sad fact that corruption "has worn the face of both Republicans and Democrats over the years." He ended that same speech by recognizing how dishonesty and manipulation in politics at a national level can reach into the lives of everyday Americans:

> No republic can permanently endure when its politics are corrupt and base...We can afford to differ on the currency, the tariff, and foreign policy, but we cannot afford to differ on the question of honesty. There is a soul in the community, a soul in the nation, just exactly as there is a soul in the individual; and exactly as the individual hopelessly mars himself if he lets his conscience be dulled by the constant repetition of unworthy acts, so the nation will hopelessly blunt the popular conscience if it permits its public men continually to do acts which the nation in its heart of hearts knows are acts which cast discredit upon our whole public life.

★ ★ ★ ★ ★

As a member of the Foreign Relations Committee, Obama traveled to Russia with Republican Senator Richard Lugar and authored a nuclear nonproliferation initiative designed to limit the number of nuclear weapons and other weapons of mass destruction in the world and keep them out of the hands of terrorists. First introduced in November 2005 and enacted in 2007, the Lugar-Obama initiative enhances U.S. efforts to destroy conventional weapons stockpiles and to detect and interdict weapons and materials of mass destruction throughout the world. It also provides U.S. funding and expertise to help the former Soviet Union safeguard and dismantle its enormous stockpiles of nuclear, chemical, and biological weapons, as well as the related materials and delivery systems. The many accomplishments of this program include the deactivating of 7,000 nuclear warheads and the reemployment of 58,000 scientists in peaceful research.

During a highly publicized trip to Africa in 2006, Obama visited a number of countries, including his father's homeland of Kenya, to promote awareness of the situation in that broken continent. He publicly took an HIV test in Kenya, visited refugee camps on the Sudan-Chad border, and met with leaders in South Africa. He has been one of the most vocal politicians on the plight of Darfur, and coauthored the Darfur Peace and Accountability

Act with Republican Senator Sam Brownback. Obama also helped secure $20 million for the African Union peace-keeping mission, and has spoken publicly against Zimbabwe's corruption under President Mugabe's regime. He has also made global poverty a key issue, working with fellow Senators Chuck Hagel and Maria Cantwell on the Global Poverty Act, which highlights an ambitious aim of cutting the world's extreme poverty in half by 2015 through a comprehensive program of aid, debt relief, trade, and co-ordination among members of the international communities, businesses, and nongovernmental organizations.

Obama's contribution to Homeland Security has focused primarily on the securities of communities and preventive measures against terrorism and national disasters. National water source security and the responsible disposal of nuclear waste top the list of his legislative concerns. He has also proposed the creation of a national family locator system in the case of an emergency caused either by a natural catastrophe or an act of terrorism.

Also of note during Obama's years in the Senate was the October 2006 publication of his second book, *The Audacity of Hope: Thoughts On Reclaiming the American Dream.* The book's title is taken from Obama's famed keynote address at the Democratic National Convention in 2004:

Hope—Hope in the face of difficulty. Hope in the face of uncertainty. The audacity of hope! In the end, that is God's greatest gift to us, the bedrock of this nation. A belief in things not seen. A belief that there are better days ahead.

While Obama's first book, *Dreams from My Father,* was primarily a personal memoir of the author's struggle to reconcile his childhood, his father's absence, and the color of his skin, *The Audacity of Hope* can be viewed more as a political biography. The new book, which received favorable reviews, is laden with his personal policy beliefs—criticizing George W. Bush for a deceptive and poorly planned war in Iraq, addressing welfare and the escalating energy crisis, and even berating other Democrats for becoming "the party of reaction." In one sense, *The Audacity of Hope* can be understood as a blueprint of Barack Obama's campaign for the U.S. presidency, which he would launch on the steps of the Illinois state capitol building just a few months after the book's release.

A HISTORIC PRESIDENTIAL CAMPAIGN

The way to continue our fight now to accomplish the goals for which we stand is to take our energy, our passion, our strength, and do all we can to help elect Barack Obama.

—HILLARY CLINTON

Much has been written about the extraordinary nature of the 2008 Democratic presidential primaries. Hillary Clinton broke an enormous gender barrier, winning more primaries and delegates than any other female candidate in American history. Bill Richardson became the first prominent Hispanic American candidate to run for any major party's presidential nomination. An unprecedented spike in voter turnout took place, with precincts running short on ballots and poll hours extended throughout the country. A country often accused of cynicism and disinterest was inspired by stories of voters packing inside community centers and local churches.

The mechanics of Barack Obama's march to the Democratic nomination for president are surprisingly simple. He ran as a candidate of change, urging people to believe in their own ability to bring about the improvements they desired. His campaign blazed new trails in terms of connecting with young people, utilizing the power of the Internet and a network of young activists across the country. Obama's campaign was also notable for its efforts in recovering the connection between faith communities and the Democratic Party.

Over the course of the campaign, Obama emphasized the issues of ending the Iraq War, increasing energy independence, and providing universal health care. As improbable as the journey has been, Obama's campaign has been remarkable for its consistent approach, even in the midst of a war on two fronts and economic disruptions.

On February 10, 2007, Obama stood on the steps of the Old Capitol Building in Springfield, Illinois, to announce his candidacy for the Democratic nomination for president in 2008:

> It was here, in Springfield, where North, South, East and West come together, that I was reminded of the essential decency of the American people—where I came to believe that through this decency, we can build a more hopeful America. And that is why, in the shadow of the Old State Capitol, where Lincoln once

called on a divided house to stand together, where common hopes and common dreams still live, I stand before you today to announce my candidacy for president of the United States of America.

Now listen, I recognize there is a certain presumptuousness—a certain audacity—to this announcement. I know I haven't spent a lot of time learning the ways of Washington. But I've been there long enough to know that the ways of Washington must change.

The genius of our founders is that they designed a system of government that can be changed. And we should take heart, because we've changed this country before. In the face of tyranny, a band of patriots brought an Empire to its knees. In the face of secession, we unified a nation and set the captives free. In the face of Depression, we put people back to work and lifted millions out of poverty. We welcomed immigrants to our shores, we opened railroads to the west, we landed a man on the moon, and we heard a King's call to let justice roll down like water, and righteousness like a mighty stream.

Each and every time, a new generation has risen up and done what's needed to be done. Today we are

> called once more—and it is time for our generation
> to answer that call.
>
> For that is our unyielding faith—that in the face of
> impossible odds, people who love their country can
> change it.

The campaign staff that Obama assembled drew heavily from his network of Chicago friends, as well as the community organizers who were his colleagues throughout the nation. The campaign focused much of its attention on the caucus that took place in Iowa in early January 2008, commonly recognized as the first step in the U.S. presidential nomination process. With the support of more than 100 young people who worked in Iowa for more than 9 months, Obama's surprising 8 percent victory in the Iowa caucus allowed him to break away from the pack of 11 Democratic challengers.

Over the rest of January 2008, the Obama campaign traded a series of close election wins with the expected Democratic Party frontrunner, Hillary Clinton. Many political experts had assumed that the Democratic presidential candidate would be decided conclusively on "Super Tuesday," February 5, when 13 states had their primaries or caucuses. Yet the race held tight, confounding expectations. Obama had great success in large rural states, while Clinton was nearly as dominant in high-population coastal areas. But in the weeks that followed Super Tuesday, Obama was able to establish a clear edge in delegate count—winning all 11 of the remaining states that were decided in February.

In March a controversy broke out involving Obama's former pastor of 20 years, Jeremiah Wright. Pastor Wright had served for more than 30 years at Chicago's Trinity United Church of Christ, the inner city megachurch of 10,000 members where Barack and Michelle were married back in 1992. After ABC News broadcast portions of Pastor Wright's sermons that included controversial statements about race in the United States, concern was raised about the degree to which Wright's statements were representative of Obama's thinking. Obama initially responded by defending Wright, and delivered a speech of his own addressing race that was titled "A More Perfect Union." In a segment of this much-praised speech, Obama spoke to the historic struggle America has had with the issue of race:

> As William Faulkner once wrote, "The past isn't dead and buried. In fact, it isn't even past." We do not need to recite here the history of racial injustice in this country. But we do need to remind ourselves that so many of the disparities that exist in the African-

American community today can be directly traced to inequalities passed on from an earlier generation that suffered under the brutal legacy of slavery and Jim Crow.

After his pastor continued to speak out, Obama condemned his remarks and ended Wright's relationship with the campaign. In a move unprecedented in U.S. presidential campaigns, Obama would go on to resign from Trinity United Church "to avoid the impression that I endorse the entire range of opinions expressed at that church."

Again confounding expectations, Obama was able to bounce back from this controversy. After Obama won the North Carolina primary held May 6, Democratic party leaders known as "superdelegates" began to endorse Obama in greater numbers. At the end of May, a win in Oregon gave Barack Obama an absolute majority of the pledged delegates. On June 3, the day of the final primary contests of Montana and South Dakota, Obama was projected to surpass the 2,118 delegates required for the Democratic nomination. Four days later, Hillary Clinton ended her campaign and endorsed Obama, declaring, "The way to continue our fight now to accomplish the goals for which we stand is to take our energy, our passion, our strength and do all we can to help elect Barack Obama."

★ ★ ★ ★ ★

After securing the Democratic Party's nomination, Obama traveled in July 2008 to Afghanistan, Iraq, Kuwait, Jordan, the West Bank, Israel, Germany, France, and Great Britain. During the course of this trip he met with U.S. military leaders and the brave men and women serving in the armed forces as well as a wide variety of international leaders. He ended this much-publicized trip with a speech before a crowd of more than 200,000 people in Berlin, Germany. In his speech, Obama spoke to the hopes and challenges for America and the world:

> I love America. I know that for more than two centuries, we have strived—at great cost and great sacrifice—to form a more perfect union; to seek, with other nations, a more hopeful world. Our allegiance has never been to any particular tribe or kingdom— indeed, every language is spoken in our country; every culture has left its imprint on ours; every point of view is expressed in our public squares. What has always united us—what has always driven our people; what drew my father to America's shores— is a set of ideals that speak to aspirations shared by all people: That we can live free from fear and free from want; that we can speak our minds and assemble with whomever we choose and worship as we please.

> Just the very fact that he's a black man. That is groundbreaking. It will disrupt things to a certain degree. It holds great potential for real change.

—ALEXANDER KAPLAN-REYES, COLLEGE STUDENT

These are the aspirations that joined the fates of all nations in this city. These aspirations are bigger than anything that drives us apart. It is because of these aspirations that the airlift began. It is because of these aspirations that all free people—everywhere—became citizens of Berlin. It is in pursuit of these aspirations that a new generation—our generation—must make our mark on the world.

People of Berlin—and people of the world—the scale of our challenge is great. The road ahead will be long. But I come before you to say that we are heirs to a struggle for freedom. We are a people of improbable hope. With an eye toward the future, with resolve in our hearts, let us remember this history, and answer our destiny, and remake the world once again.

On August 23, 2008, Obama selected Delaware Senator Joe Biden as his vice presidential running mate. Later that month, at the Democratic National Convention in Denver, Colorado, Obama's chief rival in the Democratic primaries, Hillary Clinton, gave a speech in strong support of Obama's candidacy. A day later at the convention, Clinton was the person who called for Obama to be nominated by acclamation as the Democratic presidential candidate. On August 28, Obama accepted the nomination in front of 84,000 supporters in Denver and over 38 million television viewers throughout the United States.

★ ★ ★ ★ ★

It is difficult to describe where Obama's improbable arc to victory began. Was it in Hawaii during his childhood? Was it in the streets of Chicago, or the hallowed halls of Harvard Law School? Was it in Springfield during his time as a state senator or in some strategic meeting with campaign leaders like David Plouffe, Penny Pritzker, or David Axelrod? For many, the genesis of this truly American story is revealed in a speech Obama gave at a 2006 conference of Christian community organizers, pastors, and faith leaders. Obama began his speech to the 2006 Call to Renewal conference by grounding his work as an elected official in the bedrock of America's faith:

This religious tendency is not simply the result of successful marketing by skilled preachers or the draw of popular megachurches. In fact, it speaks to a hunger that's deeper than that—a hunger that goes beyond any particular issue or cause.

Each day, it seems, thousands of Americans are going about their daily rounds—dropping off the kids at school, driving to the office, flying to a business meeting, shopping at the mall, trying to stay on their diets—and they're coming to the realization that something is missing. They are deciding that their work, their possessions, their diversions, their sheer busyness, is not enough.

They want a sense of purpose, a narrative arc to their lives. They're looking to relieve a chronic loneliness, a feeling supported by a recent study that shows Americans have fewer close friends and confidants than ever before. And so they need an assurance that somebody out there cares about them, is listening to them—that they are not just destined to travel down that long highway toward nothingness.

Obama had worked with fellow community organizers like the ones gathered for this conference for much of his faith life. He counts Jim Wallis, the founder of Call to Renewal, as a personal friend and mentor. It was the very work that activists like these folks were doing that had driven Obama to pursue politics as an avenue for creating profound and lasting change.

Obama continued in this speech to express his belief that the church is the wellspring for any lasting progress:

> You need to come to church in the first place precisely because you are first of this world, not apart from it. You need to embrace Christ precisely because you have sins to wash away—because you are human and need an ally in this difficult journey.
>
> It was because of these newfound understandings that I was finally able to walk down the aisle of Trinity United Church of Christ on 95th Street in the South Side of Chicago one day and affirm my Christian faith. It came about as a choice, and not an epiphany. I didn't fall out in church. The questions I had didn't magically disappear. But kneeling beneath that cross on the South Side, I felt that I heard God's spirit beckoning me. I submitted myself to his will, and dedicated myself to discovering his truth.

He continued by speaking about the essential link between faith and values that's at the heart of the faith of so many Americans:

> That's a path that has been shared by millions upon millions of Americans—evangelicals, Catholics, Protestants, Jews, and Muslims alike; some since birth, others at certain turning points in their lives. It is not something they set apart from the rest of their beliefs and values. In fact, it is often what drives their beliefs and their values.
>
> And that is why, if we truly hope to speak to people where they're at—to communicate our hopes and values in a way that's relevant to their own—then as progressives, we cannot abandon the field of religious discourse.

The progressive wing of U.S. politics has been criticized for lacking respect or affinity for the faith so many Americans hold. Much has been made of the perceived "God gap" in the 2000 and 2004 presidential elections in which the vast majority of professing evangelical Christians voted for Republican candidates. Yet this gap has not been the story of Obama's career in public service. His first job as a community organizer was with churches. His seminal experience of change as a young person was the civil rights movement, which drew its strength and leadership largely from the black church. As an adult, Obama spent years working side by side with Christian leaders like Rick Warren and T.D. Jakes. In front of an audience of friends, Obama spoke about the essential connection he sees between social transformation and spiritual transformation:

> Solving these problems will require changes in government policy, but it will also require changes in hearts and a change in minds. I believe in keeping guns out of our inner cities, and that our leaders must say so in the face of the gun manufacturers' lobby—but I also believe that when a gangbanger shoots indiscriminately into a crowd because he feels somebody disrespected him, we've got a moral problem. There's a hole in that young man's heart— a hole that the government alone cannot fix.
>
> I believe in vigorous enforcement of our nondiscrimination laws. But I also believe that a transformation of conscience and a genuine commitment to diversity on the part of the nation's CEOs could bring about quicker results than a battalion of lawyers. They have more lawyers than us anyway.
>
> I think that we should put more of our tax dollars into educating poor girls and boys. I think that the work

that Marian Wright Edelman has done all her life is absolutely how we should prioritize our resources in the wealthiest nation on earth. I also think that we should give them the information about contraception that can prevent unwanted pregnancies, lower abortion rates, and help assure that every child is loved and cherished.

But, you know, my Bible tells me that if we train a child in the way he should go, when he is old he will not turn from it. So I think faith and guidance can help fortify a young woman's sense of self, a young man's sense of responsibility, and a sense of reverence that all young people should have for the act of sexual intimacy.

In this speech, Obama can be seen as laying out what many see as a sort of "third way" between the radical ends of theocracy and secular humanism. Obama's ability to maintain a fragile tension between these two warring camps has been central to his rise in prominence on the U.S. political scene.

Obama is only one of millions in the U.S. and the world who yearn for this third way. You can see this hunger in the tribes of unchurched or de-churched people seeking meaning outside of stained glass and steeple structures, in "non-holy" places like coffee shops, labyrinths, festivals, and pubs. You can see this in the countless new expressions of faith communities and technology start-ups that attract young people all around the globe.

Obama asked one of the many artists in this emerging majority to lead the benediction on the first night of the Democratic Party convention that formalized his nomination. Donald Miller, a fatherless son who grew up in a transforming experience of youth ministry, and who has written books that assure so many that they are not alone, walked to the podium at the Pepsi Center on August 25. He asked the crowd to bow their heads as he prayed:

> Father God,
>
> This week, as the world looks on, help the leaders in this room create a civil dialogue about our future.
>
> We need you, God, as individuals and also as a nation. We need you to protect us from our enemies, but also from ourselves, because we are easily tempted toward apathy.
>
> Give us a passion to advance opportunities for the least of these, for widows and orphans, for single moms and children whose fathers have left. Give us the eyes to see them, and the ears to hear them, and hands willing to serve them. Help us serve people,

not just causes. And stand up to specific injustices rather than vague notions.

Give those in this room who have power, along with those who will meet next week, the courage to work together to finally provide health care to those who don't have any, and a living wage so families can thrive rather than struggle.

Help us figure out how to pay teachers what they deserve and give children an equal opportunity to get a college education. Help us figure out the balance between economic opportunity and corporate gluttony.

We have tried to solve these problems ourselves but they are still there. We need your help.

Father, will you restore our moral standing in the world?

A lot of people don't like us but that's because they don't know the heart of the average American. Will you give us favor and forgiveness, along with our allies around the world?

Help us be an example of humility and strength once again.

Lastly, father, unify us. Even in our diversity help us see how much we have in common. And unify us not just in our ideas and in our sentiments—but in our actions, as we look around and figure out something we can do to help create an America even greater than the one we have come to cherish.

God we know that you are good. Thank you for blessing us in so many ways as Americans.

I make these requests in the name of your son, Jesus, who gave his own life against the forces of injustice. Let him be our example. Amen.

Miller's prayer reiterates the problems and issues that Obama and his supporters hope to address, and asks God to aid in this fight for the good—to guide and keep those who lead humble lives in constant awe of the human spirit and their greater purpose.

Obama echoed many of the same themes in his own speech before the Democratic National Convention just four days later. Speaking on the 45th anniversary of Martin Luther King Jr.'s "I Have a Dream" speech, Obama looked forward to the promise he foresees:

(It is the) American spirit—that American promise—that pushes us forward even when the path

I think those like me who came of age during the Bush administration developed a warped view of government. After the Iraq War, the failure of No Child Left Behind, the Patriot Act, and countless other events, we now tend to view the government as something against us rather than something that supports us. This is why Obama's message of change and hope has resonated so strongly with us. He has promised that the recent failure of government will not continue when he is elected president, and this is extremely reassuring to those of us that have only seen the government make an endless string of bad decisions.

—AMY MCDONOUGH, COLLEGE STUDENT & CO-CHAIR OF OCCIDENTAL COLLEGE STUDENTS FOR OBAMA

is uncertain; that binds us together in spite of our differences; that makes us fix our eye not on what is seen, but what is unseen, that better place around the bend.

That promise is our greatest inheritance. It's a promise I make to my daughters when I tuck them in at night, and a promise that you make to yours—a promise that has led immigrants to cross oceans and pioneers to travel west; a promise that led workers to picket lines, and women to reach for the ballot.

And it is that promise that 45 years ago today, brought Americans from every corner of this land to stand together on a Mall in Washington, before Lincoln's Memorial, and hear a young preacher from Georgia speak of his dream. The men and women who gathered there could've heard many things. They could've heard words of anger and discord. They could've been told to succumb to the fear and frustration of so many dreams deferred.

But what the people heard instead—people of every creed and color, from every walk of life—is that in America, our destiny is inextricably linked. That together, our dreams can be one. "We cannot walk alone," the preacher cried. "And as we walk, we must make the pledge that we shall always march ahead. We cannot turn back."

A CALL TO ACTION

I am running for President, right now, because of what Dr. King called the fierce urgency of now. This moment is too important to sit on the sidelines.

—BARACK OBAMA

Barack Obama is running for the top office in the land on the basis of a bold belief: That change begins at ground level, and climbs from those deep roots up the power tree to the highest branches. And throughout his campaign he has called all Americans—men and women; young and old; Republicans, Democrats, and Independents; people of all races and ethnic backgrounds—to take action, to not sit idly by with a vague notion that somebody else will fix the problems in our neighborhoods, towns, cities, states, and the nation as a whole. He seeks office not out of some inflated hubris, but rather out of humility—having learned early in his days as a community organizer that to lead is to serve.

He began his life in Hawaii, the son of an idealistic young Kansas woman and a Kenyan man seeking a better way of life. From a youth spent in conflict and constant contemplation to a determination to help rally those who assumed their voices were weak and powerless, Obama labored diligently to better himself so he might also better the greater community around him. New York to Chicago's South Side in a beat-up car. Chicago to Boston in another old automobile. From Harvard Law School back to the South Side, as he had promised, to assist the disaffected folks he'd met there.

Then, he launched into a political life dedicated to directing the changes that needed to be made. First, as a state senator for his poor Chicago district, then a whirlwind leap into the U.S. Senate, and now a historic campaign for the presidency. Senator Hillary Clinton has spoken of cracking the proverbial glass ceiling for women, but Obama has, in fact, shattered that ceiling for African Americans time and time again—from becoming the first African-American editor of the *Harvard Law Review* to becoming only the third Black U.S. senator since Reconstruction. And now he will be the first African American ever to make it to a U.S. presidential General Election.

Senator Obama's primary purpose, as it has been for most of his life, is to represent and enact a process of change in both America and abroad. As can be seen from his legislative record, he strives to put integrity and high ethical standards back into the country's capital. He aims to help solve what he calls the "moral crisis" of climate change, understanding that citizens have a principle obligation to care for God's creation and to make the world safe for every single human on this earth. Drafting plans to deter the construction of nuclear arms and other weapons of mass destruction, he calls for a united effort of nations to work together to ensure lives are not lost needlessly.

As a father of two young girls, and a man who relied heavily upon scholarships, grants, and loans to finance his world-class education, Obama has sought (and continues to seek) educational reform, from kindergarten classrooms to college classrooms. Ensuring that American children receive the best schooling possible has been a priority, as has passing legislation to expand the amount of money that college students can receive from the government. Obama recognizes that America's potential for the future relies upon innovation—and the prospect of innovation depends heavily upon education and research. As Senator Obama concluded in the September 26, 2008, Presidential debate with Republican nominee John McCain:

> And part of what we need to do, what the next president has to do—and this is part of our judgment, this is part of how we're going to keep America safe—is to send a message to the world that we

are going to invest in issues like education, we are going to invest in issues that relate to how ordinary people are able to live out their dreams.

More than four decades ago, Martin Luther King Jr. called his fellow Americans to action, summoning them to seize upon a moment in history in which people of all races were willing to stand up and call for an end to discrimination, an end to corruption, and an end to violence against other human beings. He called for the leadership of America to embrace a radical reform of love and servanthood, rejecting hate and greed. The movement King led then relied heavily upon the youth of the country, who were not mired by the cynicism and rigidity of old ways and could instead conceive of a new hope on the horizon. It was a movement organized by people—ordinary people, black and white, marching through streets in unity and writing letters to leaders. And the work of these people produced real and lasting change.

Today, a zeitgeist pervades an America not too different from the one Martin Luther King spoke to from a pulpit in New York City in 1967. Young people are once again rallying for and seeking a new dawn. With bold hope, they've chosen a leader who echoes many of King's ideas and beliefs for a brighter day for all Americans. As a young man, Barack Obama read King's words and about his life, and embarked upon a calling to retrace King's steps—and forge his own path of change. Echoing King's words, he calls all to seize hope with both hands and not be afraid of idealism—because idealism paired with careful, pragmatic planning may yield incredible results.

On July 2, 2008, Obama gave a speech about civil service to a group in Colorado Springs, Colorado. During the course of his address, he echoed Martin Luther King Jr.'s fiery words spoken from that New York City pulpit 41 years prior. He appointed a passionate call to action, and summed up his reasons for running. Despite his critics, despite his own humble concession that he knows full well that he is not a perfect man and cannot promise to be a perfect president, he gave his audience an ardent argument for his candidacy—a reason to put some small faith in his vision and eagerly join the fight for a better America, a better tomorrow:

> I am running for president, right now, because of what Dr. King called the fierce urgency of now. This moment is too important to sit on the sidelines. Our country faces determined enemies abroad, and definitive challenges at home. But I have no doubt

that in the face of these odds, people who love their country can change it. That is why I am running for president. That is why I'm determined to reach out—not just to Democrats, but to Independents and Republicans who want to move in a new direction. And that is why I won't just ask for your vote as a candidate—I will ask for your service and your active citizenship when I am president of the United States.

The challenges we face today—war and poverty, joblessness and homelessness, violent streets and crumbling schools—are not simply technical problems in search of a 10-point plan. They are moral problems, rooted in both societal indifference and individual callousness—in the imperfections of man.

—SPEECH TO THE ST. LOUIS AME CONFERENCE, JUNE 5, 2008

★ ★ ★ ★ ★

And so the values we believe in—empathy and justice and responsibility to ourselves and our neighbors—these cannot only be expressed in our churches and our synagogues, but in our policies and in our laws.

—SPEECH TO THE ST. LOUIS AME CONFERENCE, JUNE 5, 2008

People are coming together around a simple truth—that we are all connected, that I am my brother's keeper; I am my sister's keeper.

— "A POLITICS OF CONSCIENCE" SPEECH, HARTFORD, CONNECTICUT, JUNE 23, 2007

★ ★ ★ ★ ★

We need to heed the biblical call to care for "the least of these" and lift the poor out of despair.

—"A POLITICS OF CONSCIENCE," JUNE 23, 2007

★ ★ ★ ★ ★

There is real evil and hardship and pain and suffering in the world and we should be humble in our belief that we can eliminate them. But we shouldn't use our humility as an excuse for inaction.

—"A POLITICS OF CONSCIENCE," JUNE 23, 2007

BARACK OBAMA ★ an american story

I'm hearing from evangelicals who may not agree with progressives on every issue but agree that poverty has no place in a world of plenty; that hate has no place in the hearts of believers; and that we all have to be good stewards of God's creations.

—"A POLITICS OF CONSCIENCE," JUNE 23, 2007

★ ★ ★ ★ ★

We all have the capacity to do justice and show mercy; to treat others with dignity and respect; and to rise above what divides us and come together to meet those challenges we can't meet alone.

—"A POLITICS OF CONSCIENCE," JUNE 23, 2007

★ ★ ★ ★ ★

If we can embrace a common destiny— then I believe we'll not just help bring about a more hopeful day in America, we'll not just be caring for our own souls, we'll be doing God's work here on earth.

—"A POLITICS OF CONSCIENCE," JUNE 23, 2007

In Other Words

For decades we've had politicians in Washington who talk about family values, but we haven't had policies that value families.

—SPEECH TO WORKING WOMEN, ALBUQUERQUE, NEW MEXICO, JUNE 23, 2008

★ ★ ★ ★ ★

There are more fundamental reasons to care. Reasons related to our own humanity. Reasons of the soul. Like no other illness, AIDS tests our ability to put ourselves in someone else's shoes—to empathize with the plight of our fellow man.

—SPEAKING AT SADDLEBACK CHURCH ON WORLD AIDS DAY, DECEMBER 1, 2006

★ ★ ★ ★ ★

We can embrace another tradition of politics... a tradition based on the simple idea that we have a stake in one another—and that what binds us together is greater than what drives us apart.

—SADDLEBACK CHURCH, WORLD AIDS DAY, DECEMBER 1, 2006

If I'm acting in an ethical way, if I am working to make sure that I am applying what I consider to be a core value of Christianity, but also a core value of all great religions, and that is that I am my brother's keeper and I am my sister's keeper, then I will be doing my part to move his agenda forward.

—DEMOCRATIC CANDIDATES COMPASSION FORUM, MESSIAH COLLEGE, APRIL 13, 2008

★ ★ ★ ★ ★

What I think we can do is to act in ways that are consummate with the values that we cherish. And sometimes that's harder to do in politics than it should be. But I think that's what's demanded of us.

—COMPASSION FORUM, MESSIAH COLLEGE, APRIL 13, 2008

★ ★ ★ ★ ★

The more I learn about the world, the more I know about science, the more I'm amazed about the mystery of this planet and this universe. And it strengthens my faith as opposed to weakens it.

—COMPASSION FORUM, MESSIAH COLLEGE, APRIL 13, 2008

Part of what my religious faith teaches me is to take an intergenerational view, to recognize that we are borrowing this planet from our children and our grandchildren...We have to find resources in ourselves that allow us to make those sacrifices where we say, you know what? We're not going to leave it to the next generation.

—COMPASSION FORUM, MESSIAH COLLEGE, APRIL 13, 2008

★ ★ ★ ★ ★

What I believe is that all of us come to the public square with our own values and our ideals and our ethics, what we believe. And people of religious faith have the same right to come to that public square with values and ideals that are rooted in their faith.

—COMPASSION FORUM, MESSIAH COLLEGE, APRIL 13, 2008

★ ★ ★ ★ ★

What religious language can often do is allow us to get outside of ourselves and mobilize around a common good.

—COMPASSION FORUM, MESSIAH COLLEGE, APRIL 13, 2008

I think America's greatest moral failure
in my lifetime has been that we still
don't abide by that basic precept in
Matthew that whatever you do for the
least of my brothers, you do for me,
and that notion of—that basic principle
applies to poverty. It applies to racism
and sexism. It applies to, you know, not
having—not thinking about providing
ladders of opportunity for people
to get into the middle class. There's
a pervasive sense, I think, that this
country, as wealthy and powerful as
we are, still don't spend enough time
thinking about the least of us.

—CIVIC FORUM, SADDLEBACK CHURCH, AUGUST 16, 2008

★ ★ ★ ★ ★

I think that we should have an all hands
on deck approach when it comes to
issues like poverty and substance abuse
and as somebody who got my start out
of college working with churches, who
are trying to deal with the devastation
of steel plants closing in the South Side
of Chicago, I know the power of faith-
based institutions to get stuff done.

—CIVIC FORUM, SADDLEBACK CHURCH, AUGUST 16, 2008

As a starting point, being a Christian means I believe in—that Jesus Christ died for my sins, and that I am redeemed through him. That is a source of strength and sustenance on a daily basis. Yes, I know that I don't walk alone. And I know that if I can get myself out of the way, that I can maybe carry out in some small way what he intends. And it means that those sins that I have on a fairly regular basis, hopefully will be washed away. But what it also means, I think, is a sense of obligation to embrace not just words, but through deeds, the expectations, I think, that God has for us. And that means thinking about the least of these. It means acting—well, acting justly, and loving mercy, and walking humbly with our God.

—CIVIC FORUM, SADDLEBACK CHURCH, AUGUST 16, 2008

BARACK OBAMA ★ an american story

To

Tenzo.

Happy Reading.

From

Tseeny.

Everyone has secrets, but you don't have to live with your pain all alone. *Secret Survivors* tells the compelling, true stories of people who've lived through painful secrets. As you read stories about rape, addiction, cutting, abuse, abortion, and more, you'll find the strength to share your own story and start healing, and you may even discover how to help a friend in pain.

Secret Survivors
Real-Life Stories to Give You Hope for Healing
Jen Howver & Megan Hutchinson
RETAIL $12.99
ISBN 978-0-310-28322-5

Visit www.planetwisdom.com or your local bookstore.

You'll laugh out loud at the embarrassing stories of Luke Lang, a self-proclaimed "freak of nature." While you're reading Luke's embarrassing stories—like the time he was beaten up by a girl in Karate class or the time he was fighting for his life at Boy Scout camp—you'll learn a little about God's love and grace, and you'll be reminded that you were created on purpose, for a purpose.

I Am Standing Up
True Confessions of a Total Freak of Nature
Luke Lang
RETAIL $9.99
ISBN 978-0-310-28325-6